1954 The girl in the cover photo is not a war victim; it is Setsuko Kusano, from her role in the **1954** Japanese movie "**Twenty-Four Eyes**" ("*Nijushi no hitomi*"). **Twenty-Four Eyes** is an excellent movie based upon the novel written by Sakae Tsuboi. It tells of the efforts of a remote island's teacher to guide her students during Japan's war years and world-wide depression with the hope they will survive. Setsuko's eyes seem trusting, thoughtful, and hopeful. Her thoughts might well be, "Will there always be wars? Can't we really do better than this?" In **1954** this writer, was released from U.S. military active duty to resume college studies at U. of IL, Chicago, at Navy Pier. Later that year I saw my first Japanese movie in a small Chicago theater; **Twenty-Four Eyes**. Remarkable!*See Notes*

The author is grateful for the permission of Shochiku Co. to use the photo of Setsuko Kusano on the cover of this book.

Castle –Romeo is the name of the hydrogen bomb explosion photo:
Credit USDOE, March 27, **1954**, Bikini Atoll, 11 Megatons.

What this book is about.

Yes, this book contains photos of victims of nuclear war. However, this book also contains a plan for world peace and the elimination of all wars.

A plan or strategy is proposed that, if adopted: would put "everyone" back to work; bring peace and stability; end war-sacrificed lives; ensure satisfactory industrial profits, growth and cooperation; and would allow people to return to peaceful opportunity-laden homelands. This **workable _moral_ strategy**, for decades or centuries to come, may be the only approach by which people of the Less Developed World _and others_, in peace, without war, can become masters of their own nation, can create a sensible path to their own peaceful destinies as people of so many other nations have done. **This workable moral strategy picks up where Einstein, Oppenheimer, and Naomi Shohno left off. It exports no United States' or other nations' money.** It prevents suicidal-self-inflicted annihilation via nuclear war, via any war. Without acting on a plan such as this the future of humanity remains very uncertain. It is affordable.

("**moral**"— concerned with the principles of right and wrong behavior and the goodness or badness of human character.)

I will hazard to believe that there are more than 7.2 Billion people on this Earth who would fully support the implementation of this plan once they learned of it and understood it. So "**Look Out**" naysayers! Get out of the way.

Do you think you would be part of the 7.2 billion? I invite you to join me in this exploration of realities for peace in this world.

Ray Wilson, Normal, IL, November, 2024

AuthorHouse™
1663 Liberty Drive
Bloomington, IN 47403
www.authorhouse.com
Phone: 833-262-8899

Because of the dynamic nature of the Internet, any web addresses or links contained in this book may have changed
since publication and may no longer be valid. The views expressed in this work are solely those of the author and do
not necessarily reflect the views of the publisher, and the publisher hereby disclaims any responsibility for them.

Any people depicted in stock imagery provided by Getty Images are models,
and such images are being used for illustrative purposes only.
Certain stock imagery © Getty Images.

This book is printed on acid-free paper.

ISBN: 979-8-8230-3844-7 (sc)
ISBN: 979-8-8230-3846-1 (hc)
ISBN: 979-8-8230-3845-4 (e)

Library of Congress Control Number: 2024926113

Print information available on the last page.

Published by AuthorHouse 01/21/2025

author HOUSE

THE Incentivization of World Peace:

Hiroshima, Nagasaki, and Nuclear War

Raymond G. Wilson, Ph.D.
Emeritus Associate Professor of Physics
Illinois Wesleyan University

Contents

"Around that time not a single person expected that I would survive. Every morning doctors came to see me and whispered, "He is still alive." I learned later that my family was prepared to hold a funeral for me. . . . I will continue to speak out for the elimination of nuclear weapons with all the strength of life in me." — Sumiteru Taniguchi [1]

Introduction

Sumiteru Taniguchi, age 16 on Thursday, August 9, 1945, was about one mile away from the Nagasaki hypocenter. A mile away from this small primitive nuclear bomb was not far enough. It was 11:02 A.M.;

Taniguchi-san was on his red bicycle delivering telegrams and post in the Sumiyoshi-machi area on that hot Nagasaki day. He was badly burned on his back, left arm, and on his buttocks, at one mile. He spent 21 months lying on his stomach in the hospital; it became his eating place and his toilet place. Repeatedly, Sumiteru pleaded with his doctors and nurses, "Kill me! Kill me!" Taniguchi-san spent most of his life warning people that the survival of humanity is threatened by the existence of nuclear weapons.[1] He died of cancer, August 30, 2017, at age 88. **Photo: R. Wilson and Sumiteru Taniguchi, 2015.** His last message to the world is here: 2 minutes long: **https://www.youtube.com/watch?v=l2DQaAz-Xvo** . If you would like his story, recorded earlier, it is here: **https://www.youtube.com/watch?v=ACu4prtWXpc** .

Photo Inset: The original inset picture is a black and white photograph of Sumiteru Taniguchi taken by U.S. Marine Sergeant Joe O'Donnell, 37 days after the bombing, September 15, 1945, in Nagasaki. Sgt. O'Donnell waved away the flies and gently brushed out the maggots before taking the picture, and then decided to take no more pictures of burn victims unless ordered to do so.

Taniguchi-kun, 1942, age 13.

Nuclear War and Its Aftermath

In 1999 a then recent Gallup Poll suggested that one in four Americans did not know that an atomic bomb had been dropped on Japan, let alone what happened after it exploded. Now, 2024, some 25 years after 1999, are Americans any better informed? My community has a population very roughly half that of 1945-Hiroshima's. *I have the feeling*, partly due to the fact that the *destructiveness of war* has never physically touched our town, that if a 2024 nuclear bomb exploded in the center of this community, most of *my* neighbors, we are about 3 miles from the population center, most would *expect* to look up and think, "What was that noise?" With 2024 nuclear weapons, after such an explosion, my town would no longer exist, and I and my neighbors would not have had time to even have such a questioning thought. Why am *I* writing this proposal rather than an American statesman? It seems rather odd that this following text originates in the town of Normal, Illinois rather than Washington, D.C. or Moscow or Beijing. When was the last time you heard about world peace plans from Washington? What is sorely needed is a workable strategy for achieving a world at peace. The U.S., the most militarily powerful nation we are told, involves itself in most wars in the world, with military budgets of hundreds of billions of dollars, and yet world peace eludes us. With a United States military or covert presence in about 140 world nations it is easy to export war. But it is contrary to all peoples of all nations' desires to create or import peace.

Mark Twain noted, "Sometimes I wonder whether the world is being run by smart people who are putting us on or by imbeciles who really mean it." That's what Mark said.

August 6, 1945 in Hiroshima: The sun was rising, only a few clouds, prospects for a good day ahead; but August in Japan — this was likely to be a hot day. People, with quiet thoughts to themselves and of family members who had emigrated to Hawaii and the United States, some, very hungry, were optimistically expecting the war to end soon.

That Day: August 6, 1945, Monday, at 8:15 A.M. in Japan: In the center of Hiroshima, just above Shima Hospital and the Kamiyacho community, it seemed like the sun had descended to the earth, followed by the heavens blasting down in a Richter-10-like cosmic quake from the gods, "rattling the earth's axis," scorching, searing, irradiating, and crushing everything and everyone below. It was as if the sun touched Hiroshima, burning people and igniting their clothing; the city became a blazing inferno with no escape for most. Neutron radiation from the bomb created radioactive phosphorus-32 from the sulfur in peoples' bones. Blast winds were in excess of 200 mph. The blast overpressure ruptured ear drums, and hurled and slammed people into walls. Scorched blistered skin sloughed and peeled off their bodies, dragging on the ground as they tried to escape the city. The retinas of eyes looking up were burned. Stone and concrete buildings were fire-gutted to their cores, the blast-shattered glass window fragments sharply tearing into the bodies of those within, and without. Today's average weapon yield can be ten times the Hiroshima bomb; some warhead yields can be 60 or more times greater.

HIROSHIMA (ATOMIC) STRIK

This happened to Hiroshima citizens within seconds on August 6. Birds and butterflies never had a chance; nor did the children at 8:15 A.M. assembling outside in the many schoolyards of the city. August 7 morning Interim-Mayor Shigetada Morishita and whoever else he could find had to deal with 70,000 dead and dying under their crushed burned and burning homes and shops, and heaped and strewn all over the streets, bridges, and river banks of Hiroshima. The incapacitated burned with the city. Over the next two weeks more people would die, day and night, averaging about 160 per hour. Radioactive substances were all over the center of the city. Thirteen square kilometers of homes, stores and shops destroyed. One small primitive nuclear bomb, the equivalent explosive power of 16,000 tons of TNT (*tons, not pounds*) detonated over the city of an estimated 280,000, sent forth an enormous flood of nuclear radiation into the people below. Many of those who survived those days were plagued by radiation illness in later months and years. By Dec 31, 1945 the death toll was about 140,000 and the counting could not stop then. It included the American and Allied military prisoners in Hiroshima and (3 days later) in Nagasaki. Hiroshima as a city was mostly wiped off the earth, as you can see. More than 140,000 people, mostly civilians, most, were disposed of as ashes and smoke, while many others who sought relief and escape in the seven rivers, sank, to be washed out into Hiroshima Bay. And they were.

August, 1945. This use to be Hiroshima City. (Getty (Gamma-Keystone))

Three days later, Thursday, August 9, at 11:02 A.M., people out and about, 21,000 tons destroyed Nagasaki and its people, killing another 73,884 by year's end.. By hindsight and knowledge later gained from surviving Japanese government officials neither bomb was necessary to bring about the end of the war. Though warned by air-dropped leaflets to evacuate Hiroshima and Nagasaki, the people in these two cities were essentially trapped, much like: the citizens of Gaza in 2024, in selected towns in Israel on October 7, 2023, and those in Ukraine as Putin wages war there in violation of the UN Charter. It's what happens whenever cities are attacked; the people are trapped and the weapons are indiscriminant. Well more than 210,000 souls were killed in these two Japanese city-bombings.

August 6, 1945. Hiroshima cloud from 368 miles.

September, 1945. Here was Nagasaki, a city of people.

In the true history of nations, the mere passage of time does not alter the morality of crimes against humanity. The definition of "atrocity" does not depend upon who commits it or the reasons for so doing. Surely these two nuclear bombs stepped over the threshold of crimes against humanity. This can be called **Nuclear Insanity**

The weapons are products of our fear, our greed, our desire for power, and our stupidity. Some Japanese have an expression for this current period of human history; they call it *"the era of nuclear madness."* But Robert Oppenheimer warned us, that **the real task at hand was not nuclear weapons but the *elimination of war itself.* "We know this because in the last war, the two nations which we like to think are the most enlightened and humane in the world—Great Britain and the United States—used atomic, (i.e., nuclear) weapons against an enemy which was essentially defeated, . . . it is <u>not thinkable</u> that in any major conflict, where the very life of a nation may be at stake, these weapons will not be used, they are much too effective for that."** [2] … And we note that the next time it will not be one-sided. Next time it is very likely that there will be an **exchange** of nuclear destruction and death.

Consider this: It would be fair to say that since 1945 the United States has spent some $20,000,000,000,000 ($20 trillion, AI-Gemini agrees) on all preparations to defend the United States and our friends from the opposition. Let me put it another way: There has been spent twenty trillion dollars for preparations to destroy and kill other nations and their people with whom we disagree. Just think of all the work-earned-and-paid taxes that went into that twenty trillion, instead of being used for all phases of the betterment of mankind. Truly, that has got to be, and will never ever be, a greater act of stupidity. Oppenheimer probably understood this, naming the goal, the ***elimination of war itself***.

Perhaps you would agree with these lines from a Martin Booth novel: Later, (in Hiroshima) after unsuccessfully trying to rescue Mishima's wife from his destroyed house and just before Mishima will take his own life he says to Joe, **"Never forget that it is men who are mad, not nations.** Men make wars. Nations do not. Leaders do — who need never fight but send others to die. Politicians are the corrupt ones. They decide, but it is we, the common men — the innocent people of the race — who act for them and suffer in their place."[3]

Indeed, it is unstable maniacal and autocratic men who order their citizens to destroy cities and to arm themselves and kill the thousands seen by these madmen to be a threat to their goals. Such lunatics have insufficient wisdom and humanity to even attempt to reasonably achieve reconciliation by peaceful means. They have other goals. There can be no doubt that, those who promote the destruction and death of cities and their people, they are mad, and they can become national leaders, as obvious in 2024.

Since 1945, and before, there have been no conflicts that could have justified using nuclear weapons. International business conflicts seem to regularly arise with major trading partner China, and with Russia, usually a U.S. trading partner. Currently, 2024, some politicos speak of possible wars with North Korea or Iran or other Middle Eastern nations. There are no American politicians, no "deciders," or "dividers," *qualified* to order the use of nuclear weapons to remedy international business conflicts, conflicts, which on a nuclear scale, are trivialities. Likewise there is no single person in Russia or China or the world, nor any cabal, *qualified* to make such a decision to indiscriminately murder hundreds of thousands within seconds. It would be utter depravity. Ruthless power-hungry Madmen will blindly think otherwise. President Truman was ill-advised before his decision; he was an angry man, as were many Americans and Britons. He stopped after using two when he learned the results.

In 2024 no nation's leader, and probably very few U.S. military officers, have ever witnessed a nuclear explosion above ground. Some people have considered nuclear explosives to be useable weapons of war; after all, in 1945 the Allies actually used two which many believe ended that war. And then, during the 1946 Bikini "Able" and "Baker" nuclear tests, U.S. congressmen, invited to witness the tests, were located so far away (for their safety) that many came away naively expressive. "Like a giant firecracker," said one. Another, "In the next war I hope we don't have to throw atomic baseballs." In 2016 the U.S. president asked, of nuclear weapons, "If we have them, why can't we use them?" *That* revealed *that* president's qualifications regarding nuclear weapon use. It seemed a game wherein, "My button is bigger than theirs." He seemed to believe *he was qualified*. To place the decision responsibility *onto* a single politician is also governmental insanity. Onto a politician?!

The nuclear madness espoused by current Madmen contains the acronym, MAD, which is used for Mutual Assured Destruction. Suicidal; that's how mad they are; truly lacking rationality.

Apparently many members of the U.S. Congress and policy creators of many nations pay little heed to wiser minds. Early on after 1945, Albert Einstein in 1947, **"We can not count on the prestige or strength of any single nation to bring about international stability.**…We scientists believe that a clear and widespread understanding of the facts and implications of the atomic discoveries is indispensable to a reasonable public stand on questions of international politics. Given this understanding, men and women will recognize that *only* **international cooperation through effective institutions can ensure security against humanity's destruction."**[4]

Carroll Quigley (former Professor at Princeton, Harvard, and the School of Foreign Service at Georgetown) — "The powers of financial capitalism had a far-reaching [plan], nothing less than to create a world system of financial control *in private hands able to dominate the political system of each country and the economy of the world as a whole.*"[5] Obviously these "powers of financial capitalism" had neither the wisdom nor qualifications to seek creation of a peaceful world, a world free from wars; they sought a different goal. I wonder who Quigley had in mind.

Albert Einstein, 1949 — "The result of these developments is an oligarchy of private capital *the enormous power of which cannot be effectively checked even by a democratically organized political society* ... since the members of legislative bodies are selected by political parties, largely financed or otherwise influenced by private capitalists who, for all practical purposes, separate the electorate from the legislature, (my italics)."[6] Einstein again, "...**unless by common struggle we are capable of new ways of thinking, mankind is doomed.**"[7]

So apparently at present *we are bound* **by political thinking, much of which seems dictated by private financial interests, not human or necessarily moral interests. How true.**

In the 20th century the *annual average* **of war-killing was more than one million people.**[8] We believe a great deal of it was brought about by political thinking dictated by private financial interests or at least supported by them. Unless there are changes we can expect such slaughter to continue. But an admonition of Albert Einstein was, "We can't solve problems by using the same kind of thinking we used when we created them." **Until the war problem is solved** this world will continue training our youngest adults, men and women, to be mass murderers, to continue bloody wars until financial control of the *economy of the world is in private hands,* undoubtedly not yours. **The stupidity of people, not of policies, continues the wholesale killing.** *It is revealing* that with supposed financial control of the world economy in private hands there is still *no guarantee* that continued centuries of wars will come to an end, or that the private hands will have *successfully developed the world.* It may very well be that *the sources of many of our wars are the competitive powers of financial capitalism, run amok in some manner,* and perhaps the powers don't realize it. That need not be. Supposedly quantum computing will take over the world economy and it is yet to be determined whether it will be for the good of the world or for the good of the few. {"Policies" are inanimate; they cannot be stupid (or smart).}

New Ways of Thinking

What follows utilizes *new ways of thinking* **based upon human and moral interests, interests that would be chosen by humanitarians but not by authoritarians or militarists.** The absence of nuclear weapons is no guarantee that the world would be at peace. Before 1945 conventional armaments were in abundance, killing millions. As Oppenheimer said, **the problem is not nuclear weapons; it is "the** *elimination of war itself*". If critics find *fault* with the following proposed strategy it does not mean rejection of the strategy, it means correct the *fault*; find and employ *new ways of thinking*. Without necessary changes in behavior we face continued centuries of wars, spending all *our created-wealth* with the prospect of destroying one another and all of our advancements. **Made by stupidity, it is the worse investment in all of history, America alone in 2024, about $886,000,000,000+ per year for killing and destruction.**

Achieving and Preserving World Peace

World initiatives for action need to be taken away from the military-industrial-congressional-media-establishment complex, taken away from the war peddlers and their supporters with their insidious subversions, conspiracies, and fascistic lies, their mythological belief in their superiority and purpose, and their self-assumed destiny to dominate nations, to rule the world, or their part of the world by warfare. You can name a few of these people and their organizations. World initiatives need to be redirected, not toward wars, dominance, and conquest, but toward peace for all those nations that are ready for peace, ready for the promised advances of the 20th and 21st centuries. At present U.S. and many nations' foreign and military policies are subverted and corrupted by events abroad, corrupted often by private financial interests and by the madmen that seek great personal and private gain. National and international discourse needs redirection toward peace and away from war. For instance, schedule weekly or monthly *public transparent discussions between* nations' statespersons and among national officials, constructive, meaningful, beneficial, and insightful, so that the public could understand what is true and what generates conflicts rather than harmonious cooperation. The public will recognize falsehoods and likely have suggestions for **mutualism.**

We will propose here a *workable moral strategy* that would solve many problems the world faces, including the war problem. It is a comprehensive *alternative* approach to the most pressing domestic and foreign priorities of the world's nations. It is an *alternative* that creates advantages for the working people of the world and at the same time provides advantages to the social, industrial, financial, and defense complexes of world

nations, and it does so without "damaging" such complexes. This workable strategy *provides a remedy to unemployment throughout the world.* As will be shown, it will put back to work the original creators of the world's wealth, initially well more than millions of them, half in the United States, for starters. It will reestablish worldwide markets for peacetime manufactured products of all nations. *It will provide for creativity and peaceful advantageous productivity in all nations.*

Robert Oppenheimer, "father" of atomic bombs, told us 78 years ago in 1946, that "…**wars might** be avoided by the following actions: universal disarmament; limited national sovereignties; provision for all people of the world of: a *rising* standard of living, better education, more contact with and better understanding of others, and equal access to the technical and raw materials which are needed for improving life…"[9] Let us refer to this as "**Oppenheimer's Conjecture**." He lost his government security clearance and was no longer asked for advice, by the government. (His reputation was formally restored 55 years after he died.)

In the following, a plan or strategy is proposed that, if adopted: would put "everyone" back to work; bring peace and stability; end war-sacrificed lives; and ensure satisfactory industrial profits, growth, and cooperation; and would allow people to return to peaceful opportunity-laden homelands. This *workable moral strategy*, for decades or centuries to come, seems the only approach by which people of the Less Developed world, in peace, without war, can become masters of their own nation, can create an intelligent path to their own peaceful destinies, as so many other nations have done. **This workable moral strategy exports no United States' or other nations' money.** It fosters the expressed desires of all people and nations seeking: peace, justice, opportunity, and a better life. This strategy has been referred to by some as "brilliant." Well, certainly; the strategy incorporates ideas advocated by J. Robert Oppenheimer, Albert Einstein, Philip Morrison & Kostas Tsipis [10], Naomi Shohno [11], and James C. Warf [12], some very wise fellows. **This is the strategy that picks up where Einstein, Oppenheimer, and Shohno left off.** We describe and recommend a workable moral strategy that can be referred to as the *"incentivization"* of world peace. (The United States does not have a single, unified world peace plan; neither does Russia, China or the United Nations.) **Incentivization** *of the type to be proposed seems missing in all other plans.*

Here We Go: A Workable Moral Strategy for Achieving and Preserving World Peace

Since the United States is currently the world's major arms supplier it makes moral and economic sense that the U.S. should have part of the responsibilities for leading the way to world peace. Thus the United States would announce a strategy, that starting one year from now it will revise the manner by which it provides aid to all other nations and particularly to those of the Less Developed world, provides aid using tax-wealth created by American citizens, as can also be done by citizens of other Developed nations. This *new-revised-aid* will be considerably greater but it will no longer be *direct* aid. All other Developed nations are encouraged, invited, to similarly participate so that they would also obtain benefits that will accrue to them just as benefits will accrue to the United States and all other participating nations.

Henceforth, rather than direct aid, the United States will provide the **United Nations** with $165 billion per year in "credit chits" (promissory notes) for use by Less Developed nations. All other Developed nations are invited to contribute *in total* an additional $165 billion in "credit chits" to the UN; *more if they wish*. These promissory notes are for development tools, equipment and knowledge **only**, not for money. *No actual money transfers to any nation.* The credit chits *originating in the U.S.* will only be redeemable in cash from the United States Treasury by American businesses and industries. With cooperation from other nations it means $330 billion *or more* per year of *knowledge and material development aid* will flow to the Less Developed world, much more than is *currently provided*, a great deal of which we know under the current system is **wasted, corrupted, or spent on tools of war**. Please note: there are only about 196 nations on this earth. $330 billion divided among, say, 164 *Developing nations* means about $2 billion annually to each of, say, 164 *Developing nations*. Of course some small nations may not need $2 billion *annually*. (196 nations – 164 developing nations = 32 developed nations); ($165 billion/31 dev.-nations = $5 billion/developed nation or there-about, if we all pitch in.)

It seems affordable. On April 10, 2009 the small nation of Japan, not at war with anyone, announced a $150 billion government stimulus package. In 2009 Japan could afford to do this. $5 billion annually would be quite a stimulus in Japan! You can hear a conservative United States Congress complaining that we cannot afford to do something like that. But financial resources are always found for wars. We can be smart enough (I think.) to find resources for a peace that eliminates wars and the costs of wars. We will show reference that the workable strategy we are proposing will lead to more than 500,000 U.S. peacetime *manufacturing jobs* in the first year – with more to come, and greatly more than 500,000 other peacetime *development jobs* throughout the world. **The world will be purchasing Peace instead of wars**. (Many peace proposals seem to imply that peace would have no cost. Ha!) Each day war would become closer to annihilation and extinction, hence military spending originally for killing and destruction becomes peace spending, its Original Purpose. **We will show how war becomes eliminated.**

The United Nations makes the "credit chits" available to **peaceful *democratic* nations** of the Less Developed and Developing Worlds. Additionally, chits will also be very cautiously offered to those nations which are verifiably peacefully evolving toward equitable nondiscriminatory *constitutional democracy*. Their democracies will be self-defined, but in all cases their citizens will have the right and the ability to make changes when necessary. These chits for knowledge and development are made available to Developing nations based on *solicited application* of: development proposals from them, verifiable need, and guarantees against misuse or corruption.

These chits to be offered by the United Nations may be utilized *only for social and economic development*, six specific self-sufficiency goals:

1. modern appropriate agriculture, food, and fresh clean water production;
2. good sheltering and its basic amenities, including electricity, plumbing, sewage;
3. health care, with hospitals, clinics, electronic communication, and well-trained doctors and nurses
4. national wealth creation from their own natural and human resources and improved infrastructure and coastal infrastructure
5. civilian security, and;
6. education and training at all levels to support goals 1-6

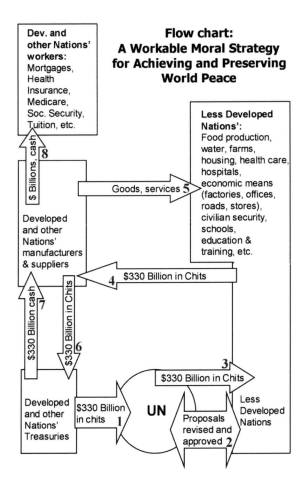

The solicited development proposals submitted to the United Nations will be carefully evaluated by experts, in terms of the proposed societal, cultural, economic, and environmental impact, and in terms of protection against abuse and corruption. The UN will aid revisions of unacceptable proposals until they are in line with this UN sanctioned, workable, and moral strategy.

Cautions

Administering this program, the United Nations **will not grant chits** to nations where war exists or is likely or where violations of rights: gender, religious, human, or ethnic, are active or not being remediated. Repressive, apartheid, and military governments and martial law governments will not qualify for participation in this program, neither will any nation, chit donor or receiver, regardless of its size, power and influence, that is not fully and **actively transparently participating and cooperating in the worldwide elimination of: armaments of war, nuclear, chemical, and biological weapons, terrorism, and the illicit drug trade. All participating nations will be in abidance with the obligations of their signature on the**

UN Charter. Eventually, the role, responsibilities, existence, and necessity of organizations like NATO would become questionable. Chits may pass through other nations on their way back to their origin nation, that is, pass through nations that also must be in abidance with the conditions of this paragraph. (It might also be possible to combine this strategy with nations' national debt obligations. Nations do write-off their war losses and expenditures; peace expenses can be written off also.) In democracies seeking peace, justice, and advancement *the people will not choose continued corruption and wars.* **The above requirements are not excessive; they are what nations have already sworn onto by their signature on the UN Charter.[13] All the above are the essential specifications to qualify for this workable moral strategy for achieving and preserving world peace.**

Less Developed nations *receiving* credit chits can expect constant on-site verification and audit by United Nations inspectors, comptrollers, and visitors. The Less Developed nations can also expect international news reporting the progress of their projects, and their failures or lack of progress.

Preferences: Preferences in the allocation of development credit chits will be given to those nations: 1) which are able to demonstrate a continuing reduction or lack of "war armament", 2) which are part of a multination cooperative regional development with other participants in this strategic program; and preference will be given to 3) nations which have instituted United Nations recommended and appropriate educational programs designed to lead their nations *peacefully* through the 21st Century. United Nations educational programs will teach ways to peace, not to conflict and war.

The chits are exchanged for the approved peacetime goods and services from the Developed nations' suppliers, the chits eventually making their way back into the Developed nation of origin; *this must happen within two years.* When the chits arrive back in the origin Developed nation they do not go to the national treasury. They go to the origin nation's makers and suppliers of the peacetime goods and services. Upon verified delivery of those goods and services and verification of their proper installation and successful operation, the chits may then be cashed in by the goods and services creators and suppliers at the origin nation's treasury, thus **enhancing wealth, productivity, and employment in the nation of chit origin.** In a year's time $165 billion or more will flow from the U.S. Treasury into the U.S. economy as wages and salaries and production costs. The U.S. creators and suppliers pay their workers and they replenish their supplies, from U.S. sources whenever possible. In the U.S. workers pay their income tax and Medicare and Social Security tax, and make payments on their home mortgages. Everyone works, everyone benefits as was meant to be in the US. It can be seen also that it would be more than foolish for a creator and supplier nation to supply goods created outside their nation. **Thus, chits can be converted to money only in the chit origin nation, the money going to the**

workers and their industries. It would make sense that wherever possible the chits should be put to work in donor nation geographic regions where there is greatest unemployment, e.g., in 2024, Puerto Rico, Rhode Island, Nevada, Michigan, Illinois, D.C., California,, etc..

Thus, each participating Developed nation annually deposits "credit chits" with the United Nations; the money actually remains in the Developed nation's treasury, until payout is due to the Developed nation's own industries and workers. **There will be great advantages to all nations who make chit deposits into this program, and considerable disadvantages to those who can, but do not. The more chits deposited, the greater economic value accrues to the depositor nation. It should be obvious.**

Also, since each Less Developed nation will be creating new productive businesses and industries, they too can become suppliers of goods outside their nation. However, their main goal is satisfying the needs of their own people, and that may well include establishing external trade relationships.

Each Less Developed nation, recipients in this program, will keep an appropriate size national militia trained for natural and other disaster service and for maintaining civil order in times of need, but not for the burden of war. With the war burden gone in the Less Developed world, their former expensive and burdensome military costs will now provide peacetime labor costs within these Less Developed nations. Factories, offices, homes, schools, hospitals, roads, farms, shopping centers, etc., must be built and staffed. Great changes could be obtainable in two years rather than twenty, and in twenty years rather than 200.

With this moral strategy there will likely be deposited with the United Nations some US$330 billion or more in credit chits. If Less Developed Nation A does not take advantage of the chits, Less Developed Nation B will, and Nation A will watch, from the sidelines.

The only way life can improve in the Less Developed world is for those nations to increase their own productivity of their lives' necessities; they need to create their own wealth, their own future as India, Sierra Leone, and China are doing in this century – the old fashioned way. Each Less Developed nation should insist on themselves creating "added value" to their natural resources (with due consideration to the societal and environmental impact) by processing such resources at home, rather than simply shipping only raw and crude materials abroad: phosphates, copper, chromium, aluminum, rare earths, diamonds, uranium, oil, minerals, etc. By this means greater wealth is created in each Less Developed nation, and will allow them much greater freedom and economic power, e.g., for additional imports from Developed nations, like the U.S.,

Japan, China, India, Germany, Russia, etc. And the Less Developed nations must plan ahead for when their natural resources are depleting.

Can leaders of democratic nations of the Less Developed world work together to make the 21st century *their* century? Would they pass up an opportunity like this? They should consider the especially appropriate example of Japan in the period 1945 to about 1970, a mountainous nation, poor in natural resources, socially and physically destroyed by war but in many ways recovering well in 25 years. Their greatest resource was their people, something that their former military government did not appreciate or protect.

Each year *this strategic, workable, and moral program* will see returned to the nonmilitary economies of the Developed nations, in total, some US$330 billion or more, to be used solely for peacetime goods and services! Hence, this proposed program should greatly reduce unemployment in any nation participating, supplier or receiver. *This program will put workers, the original creators of wealth, back on the job.* **I would estimate that the first year could create in the U.S. alone some 500,000 or more jobs.** The flow chart above illustrates this process. **Where do we get such an estimate of the number of jobs to be created or restored?**

David Swanson reported on the Internet, in RootsAction, September 9, 2011, a 2009 study by the Political Economy Research Institute at the University of Massachusetts (Amherst) (**http://rootsaction.org/news-a-views/232-i-just-found-29-million-jobs**) that estimated that $60 billion could create 193,000 jobs in the United States. Estimates were made for different kinds of jobs, clean energy, healthcare, education. If they were all in education the $60 billion would make possible some 1,050,000 jobs. I'm taking a conservative path here: If $60 billion would create 193,000 jobs then the U.S. $165 billion could create over 500,000 manufacturing jobs in the United States. I am assuming that the other $165 billion from all other participating Developed nations could create more than 500,000 manufacturing jobs in those Developed nations. Using the same reasoning, the Japanese 2009 stimulus of $150 billion could have created about 500,000 Japanese manufacturing jobs, had it been used in this manner. *That is well over one million jobs in the nations that are supplying chits.*

How many peacetime jobs will also be created in the Less Developed chit-receiving nations, where labor costs are lower? What would you guess that their former military expenditures could support for peacetime labor? *Initially more than two million?* There will no longer be money for marauding bands of revolutionaries.

Adoption of this policy means an exchange can be made: —With self-sufficiency and self-defined but true democracy *growing* in the Less Developed world and the virtual elimination there of poverty, illiteracy, malnutrition, disease, neocolonialism, rights deprivation, indebtedness, exploitation, and slavery; —The entire world could have full economic recovery, elimination of the possibility for international nuclear catastrophe, and **the practical elimination of war**. In a world at peace the refugee problem is solved. The killing stops and solutions to *worldwide* problems can be worked upon and found. The basic tool is cooperation and proper incentives, not sanctions, boycotts, and deadly threats; justified benefits, not penalties; advantages for all.

As promised, no money would leave any nation, and all the credit chits never pass through the World Bank, or any bank, or the International Monetary Fund. This moral strategy considerably modifies military spending by all nations. **If all nations are fulfilling their obligations working for peace, what need is there for *offensive* armament, nuclear bombs and missiles?** *What need would there be for military defenses.*

Each year this workable and moral program will see *returned* to the non-military economies of the Developed nations, in total, some US$330 billion or more, to be used solely for deliverance of peacetime goods and services! Hence, this proposed program should greatly reduce unemployment in any nation participating, supplier or receiver. This program will put workers, the original creators of wealth, back into manufacturing jobs, making useful products. When this plan is activated individual **citizens of participating Developed nations** would come to understand that they are active participants, **creating tools, equipment, materials, and know-how**, making possible peace and justice onto all regions of the world, and doing it without guns, bombs, drones and missiles, without destruction and killing thousands or tens of thousands.

Citizens of the Less Developed world will finally begin to see their hopes and dreams of a peaceful advancing homeland coming true. Their long sought permanent homes, employment opportunities, health care, utilities, schools, society, foods and water, secure coastlines, etc., all coming into being, and **by their own work and efforts, with the tools, equipment, materials and know-how** provided by all the participating Developed nations of the UN who committed themselves to such types of obligation with their UN Charter signature. [13] Their fear of their home being plowed under or bombed would no longer exist.

Summary I

When the "chits" are allocated the field is leveled; Less Developed nations can then negotiate with all participating Developed nations to gain the best advantage for themselves. Corruption possibility here; money under the table; "Choose my products." A sturdy constitution in a democracy should be able to handle that. Political and financial obligations to "powerful" nations become unnecessary, with no obligations to purchase military equipment from the powerful. Imperialism becomes a wasteful and useless concept. From the example of Japan's recovery from WWII, **we estimate that this specific program need continue only 25 years before modification. This author will not be available then.**

We believe all **workers of the world**: of China, Russia, Iran, Syria, India, Mozambique, Chad, Korea, Ukraine, Israel, Palestine, et al, **would greatly favor this war-ending solution, and press their leaders to accept it.** (Perhaps you noticed that the improvements sought for Less Developed nations are similar to improvements sought for certain regions and communities of *some Developed nations*. They can be included, since they are of no war threat for the people.)

Consider what 4,050,000,000 people of the Less Developed world do not have, and who is capable of supplying it! Where would they find the money? There are *abundant opportunities for all,* chit donors and receivers! This proposal has the potential of bringing together the people of possibly 196 nations for the purpose of ending wars and creating a peaceful, cooperative world. This plan is "**THE Incentivization of World Peace**." Billions of people worldwide would be able to have jobs and greatly improved lives. If you think that this approach to world peace could become quite costly, compare it to the cost of "attempting" to recover from a war that could involve the United States (and Allies) and Russia, China, and stateless terrorists. Such a war could result in hundreds of millions of deaths as well as physical destruction of the major cities on the surface of an Earth more greatly radioactive than in 2024. Costly indeed.

There are likely 8 billion people worldwide who would welcome this plan for world peace with open arms. **Support is there!** It may require new ways of thinking. But listen closely to the naysayers and from whence come their thoughts, words, and actions, and how their wealth depends upon the war and military industries, not the peace industry.. And recall that the *average annual death toll from wars* is in excess of one million.[8]

A world at peace as described above would greatly aid solution of present day social problems, in particular the immigration problems in Europe, Africa, the Middle East, the United States, and Latin America; the problems from which they flee would be solved by this strategy. They need to stay to help in the construction of their improved society. We note here also that there is a trend for families of increasing affluence to have fewer children.

One might ask whether the Developed World has any *unmet obligations* to the Less Developed World, obligations for centuries of deprivations, wars, ill-treatment, and physical, biological and sociological contamination.

Additional Requirements for the Workable Moral Strategy

We believe the following *additional* and essential requirements based upon **Oppenheimer's Conjecture** must also be employed to add facilitating strength to the workable moral strategy for a peaceful world.

Requirement 1. To further assure and advance self-determination, development, and confidence for the people of all nations it is necessary to establish government and private *international exchange programs* involving 10,000 to 50,000 people per year, students, teachers, workers, farmers, artists, government officials, scientists, athletes and upper-bracket bureaucrats; for the purpose of finding friendships, and creative new approaches to cooperation and development for mutual and world benefit.

Requirement 2. The "Sister Cities Program" should be greatly expanded to include the developing nations of the world. Timbuktu (in Mali) is a sister city with Tempe, AZ. (Look it up.) Does your town have a sister city in the Developing World? *Important question: Why, and why not?* Shall we ever be able to have sister cities in North Korea? How about Kimhyonggwon in the DPRK (North Korea)?

Requirement 3. The United Nations needs to decide when and how it can intervene in the internal affairs of a "nation." The United Nations' inability to act over past years has enabled the deaths of millions. Consider Cambodia, Rwanda, Sudan, Somalia, and now in 2024, Syria, Israel-Palestine and Ukraine. The United Nations needs to come to grips with the fact that United Nations actions—which were possible in 1946 at the creation of the UN—are woefully inadequate and much too late for events of the modern electronic and high speed world. The Cold War has changed; greater United Nations activity without vetoes should become possible. What shall be done about civil wars and "ethnic cleansings"? How many need to be killed, imprisoned, or tortured, before the United Nations shall act? 10,000? 100,000? 1,000,000? The 2006 year-end death toll in the Darfur, Sudan was estimated to be more than 100,000. Syria's is now estimated to be 580,000+ (2024). What shall be the limit before a nation is dismissed from the United Nations until its leadership is replaced, perhaps by the United Nations, and the oppressed people are empowered? **Clearly, under the world**

conditions being proposed by this workable moral strategy which would lead to modern-day democratic nations, such repression and civil wars would be highly unlikely.

Where is the voice of the United Nations General Assembly in all this? What is "world opinion" about the possibility of world peace and prosperity? The killing goes on and most of the world's people behave like zombies, plodding along, their vision constrained to their own personal needs, worries, entertainments, and desires.

Requirement 4. The United Nations <u>needs to specify the penalty</u> for any nation that employs a nuclear weapon in offense or defense. It is absolutely clear that such use would be a crime against humanity. There will be people to be found guilty, and likely retaliation, destroying weapons, not people. The International Criminal Court has issued an arrest warrant for Vladimir Putin, suspect in the unlawful transport of children from Ukraine into Russia. Switzerland's criminal code incorporates violations of international humanitarian law, including war crimes. This allows them to prosecute directly, suspected war criminals found within its territory. Switzerland recognizes the concept of universal jurisdiction, meaning they can prosecute war criminals for crimes committed elsewhere, regardless of their nationality or the location of the crime. And extradition is also a possibility.

Developing nations, yielding their military burden in favor of democracy and peaceful progress must have assurances that they will be *quickly and adequately protected*, not necessarily with military force, by the UN and the strongest powers of the world. North Korea, Iran, Israel, the U.S, and other nations need to understand what changes they need to make to receive assurances and protection against attack by any other nation. Not pre-programmed bureaucrats or dysfunctional politicians, but "Minds more wise," must speak to United Nations Charter revisions. Because all nations are not equal there should be special rules to apply to emerging, developing nations for the protection of their people from corrupt governance and from powerful outside political and exploitive influences.

We ask the reader to actually consider what would result should this workable moral strategy be offered to the United Nations, and further what would result if the membership of the United Nations agreed to its implementation.

We believe the *workers of the world*, of the Americas, of Russia, of China, of Europe, Africa, Asia, and the Middle East would approve of this plan. What a pleasant idea, to finally be at peace with our global cooperative neighbors! Unless, for some reason, a wrench is thrown into the works. It is understandable that national leaders in these democratic societies would be under considerable pressure from their citizens to accept and adhere to the stated conditions if those leaders expect to be honored in their nations' histories. This proposal has the potential to change the world for the better. It is bold and ambitious, but among the sensible nations that possess weapons of mass destruction it is achievable. We should get to it. But some nations with nuclear weapons, they will hold up the process. I don't know if any society would wish to be associated with their leadership or their economy; they are delaying the peaceful developed world. So, get out of the way, naysayers, militarists, maniacs, fascists, out of the way of the humanitarian peace-builders who know that peace can be achieved. Those who wish to solve international problems via bloody wars, please raise your hand.

For the Developed World to reject this type of plan implies that the controlling oligarchy of private capital influencing legislative bodies would much prefer to continue trying to structure a world system of financial control in private hands, through wars, financial obligations, and regime changes, with the _world's **continuing**_ _**military expenditures** well in excess of_ **$2,240,000,000,000+ (USD)** _every year, bound to increase, for the purpose of destruction and possibly killing millions, tens of thousands of children._ And here is a possible source of corruption; after _reducing_ world military expenditures, what do nations do with leftovers from their original military budgets? Obviously, since we are ending a war syndrome, the US $165 billon contribution would likely come from the present US $886 billion military budget, leaving the members of Congress to decide what to do with the remaining $721,000,000,000 Oh-oh! But in a true strong peoples' democracy the people will, I hope, choose wisely and correctly.

What you have just read is the result of this writer's attempts at new ways of thinking. We are not an "Einstein" but we believe this strategy is a considerably better approach than following some questionable leadership's demands for exclusivity of their nation's population, or their **tyrannical decrees** to destroy neighboring cities and towns and their families and children for no good reason. There is more. Thanks for getting this far. I'm tired too.

Reminding the reader: The military prediction of "Constant Conflict": ". . . There will be no peace. At any given moment for the rest of our lifetimes, there will be multiple conflicts in mutating forms around the globe. Violent conflict will dominate the headlines, but cultural and economic struggles will be steadier and ultimately more decisive. The de facto role of the US armed forces will be to keep the world safe for our economy and open to our cultural assault. To those ends, we will do a fair amount of killing. . . ." — Major Ralph Peters of the Office of the Deputy Chief of Staff for Intelligence, 1997, where he was responsible for future warfare.[14] A fair amount: — How many is that?

Naomi Shohno

And Shohno-sensei's reminder: 1986, Hiroshima: — "On the other hand we also possess the seeds of goodness and justice that humankind was given by nature and has fostered over the ages. We have the ability to cultivate self-control and consideration for others and to strive to live together in a humane and harmonious manner with others. The revival of such true humanity—not only between individuals, but also between nations—is an absolute necessity today, for the age has come when one nation's self-centered behavior could lead all humanity to annihilation." .[Naomi Shohno, THE LEGACY OF HIROSHIMA – ITS PAST, OUR FUTURE, Kosei Publishing Co., Tokyo, 1986, page 135. ISBN 4-333-01234-1 [11] (There is a similarly-titled book by Edward Teller and Allen Brown.)]

Hiroshima physicist Naomi Shohno was of the opinion that it is the responsibility of the United States *to lead the world in the direction of peace*. It seemed to him that no other nation will; it seemed to him that no other nation could. Who would even try? Russia? United Kingdom? China? Japan? Does the United States want to lead the world in the direction of peace? Shohno did not mean for the US to militarily react against every nation that gives it the "evil eye".

Ideals

Andrei Sakharov

Oh, that's way too idealistic. The "father" of the USSR's hydrogen bombs, Andrei Sakharov [15], commented on idealism, "There is a need to create ideals even when you can't see any route by which to achieve them, because if there are no ideals then there can be no hope and then one would be completely in the dark, in a hopeless blind alley." This document will provide a "route" out of our blind alley.

The above quotations from Oppenheimer imply that in 1946 he thought that the United States wanted to avoid wars. The New World Economic Order (NWEO) espoused by U.S. administrations for the past several decades suggests that different goals are sought. Consider the following even older note from Norman Dobbs: **"We are now at the year 1908**, which was the year that the Carnegie Foundation began operations. And, in that year, the trustees meeting for the first time raised a specific question, which they discussed throughout the balance of the year, in a very *learned* fashion. And the question is this: Is there any means known more effective than war, assuming you wish to alter the life of an entire people? And *they conclude* that, no more effective means to that end is known to humanity, than war. So then, in 1909, they raise the second question, and discuss it, namely, how do we involve the United States in a war?" — **https://www.globalresearch.ca/war-and-the-new-world-order/6577**

But was their "learned conclusion" correct in the first place? It seems not clear whose life is intended to be altered, those waging or fighting the war, those suffering it, or those profiting from it. Wars were different then, 1908; but the deaths were the same. I thought that in 1908 the United States was basically a Christian nation. Were the Carnegie Foundation trustees motivated by Christian principles, bright ideas and ideals? The United States NWEO is missing significant humanitarian input.

Why not take a moment to consider these two questions.

1. In the procedures that have been recommended and proposed in "THE Incentivization of World Peace" **do you see any threats to any individuals, groups, industries, corporations, or nations?**
2. In the procedures recommended and proposed, if implemented, **do you have any doubts about any of the benefits that would accrue to individuals, groups, societies, industries, corporations, nations, and the world? Would there be peace?** Has anything been overlooked?

Action Examples Re: Workable Moral Strategy

Here are some fictitious examples of the mechanics of this workable moral strategy.

Example: Tanzania, satisfying the requirement of an adequate and improving democracy, wishes to further expand its agriculture and tourism by: improved water supplies, farm machinery, improved communications, construction of tourist villages on the Mwambani Bay coast and near Ruvu Bay, and small medical clinics in some remote areas. It has found that all the materials and consultants for this development can be obtained at a good price from India, Taiwan, and Finland. These three Developed Nations have also met the conditions for participation in this moral strategy for peace.

Tanzania exchanges its United Nations granted credit chits for those goods and services from those nations. For the aid from Finland it uses chits originally from Finland. But India and Taiwan are also involved and they have requested to receive chits which originated in the U.S. and Canada. So far no money has gone anywhere. The Finnish *industries* that supplied the goods and services and verified their proper use and operation, take the chits they received and exchange them in the Finnish Government Treasury for cash, to pay their workers and replenish their supply of raw materials. No money left Finland.

The chits of U.S. and Canadian origin granted to Tanzania were given to India and Taiwan for their products, services, and verified functional operation. India and Taiwan in turn use those same chits for goods, services, and complete operational functionality from U.S. and Canadian *industries* who in turn exchange the chits at their government treasuries to pay their workers and continue their industry's growth. The workers pay income, social security, and medical care taxes and pay their mortgages. India, among other items, exchanged chits for 10 super-speed computers. Taiwan used their chits for very sophisticated medical equipment from the U.S.

Other projects: India and Bangladesh will cooperatively work on flood control projects to control the Ganges, Brahmaputra, and Meghna rivers, controlling adequate water for the fertile delta but also channeling excess water into the largest arid regions of India, and into regions in need of clean water for human consumption. And in another upcoming Indian project: Some chits will make possible the solution of the 48 year-cycle rat infestation problem in Mizoram in Northeast India, between Bangladesh and Burma. Pakistan is considering bringing fresh water from the northern mountains, in a controlled manner, to its arid regions while simultaneously creating a canal system to prevent future flooding in its plains. Heavy machinery will be required for these projects. Pakistan also wishes to establish a rural electrification project.

Many previously out-of-work people are now profitably employed. No money has left any nation. Many people in India, Taiwan, the United States, Canada, Bangladesh, Finland, and Tanzania will have productive improved lives.

(I have no idea if any of the above would be sought by Tanzania, India, Taiwan, Bangladesh; it is simply an example of how the chits could be used to create peace and to improve people's lives.)

Obviously, *IF the Peoples Republic of China is participating* in this program they will receive chits from all over the Less Developed world; China makes "everything" and makes it available at a good price. However, there are things that China needs and which it cannot yet manufacture, but things that the Developed world does manufacture. What I have in mind is sophisticated medical equipment, electronics, heavy machinery (Caterpillar), energy machinery, high technology agricultural equipment, etc. So now, *if possible*, we would have China ordering products manufactured in the U.S. and other developed nations, establishing trade relationships that would continue beyond the duration of the project, into the era without nuclear weapons, the era of peaceful collaborative relationships. China is changing; consider *all* that has evolved in China since 1949.

Kosta Tsipis   **Philip Morrison**

Morrison and Tsipis, in their book, *Reason Enough To Hope* [10], explore some of the problems facing the world should the impoverished billions of people be brought online to also benefit from "the good life" as we in the Developed world have. Food and energy needs, and overpopulation are likely to present many difficulties. Food requirements and overpopulation are of course linked. In the Japan of 120 years ago large families were common, families with four to eight and more children. In today's highly Developed Japan the "ideal" family, to maintain population, will have two children, one girl and one boy. In actuality, now in a Japanese woman's lifetime, on average, she will bear less than two children. If food and water, education, health care, peace, and economic opportunity are available, parents in a democratic society of a Less Developed nation should rather quickly learn that a family totaling four will likely do better all-around in contrast to a family of ten.

What would policy makers prefer: —$80 billion spent to support U.S.-Japan military bases in Japan, Okinawa, and elsewhere in Asia, in anticipation of conflict which could possibly never occur, —or $80+ billions to *eliminate the threats of wars* in Asia and stabilizing foreign governmental relationships, while simultaneously enhancing the lives of destitute, distressed, and sometimes oppressed people, bringing them much better life opportunities and international understanding, and steering $80+ billions into peacetime production and services from the Developed world, and fruitful cooperation and understanding of the people and wisdom of Asia?

Squabbles over tiny artificial and uninhabited islands in Asian waters can be resolved peacefully; there need be no repeat of Asian wars. Japan supports industry in China and Taiwan. China and Taiwan purchase Japan made products. Japan could benefit from oil extraction from Russian waters. The mix is much like joint ventures regardless of who "owns" the land where the ventures are ongoing. I elaborate upon this in Boulder 3, a few pages ahead. What should be the highest priority, the moral needs, the human needs, or the political "needs"? Wars' threats seem stimulated by national political "clout" and "guts" but more likely by national greed.

Boulders in the Road

Regrettably, at present, not all nations wish to live in peace with their neighbors. For a temporary period, there must be assembled, trained and *integrated*, a United Nations multinational force, **armed only if necessary**, the principle function of which shall be to *immediately* aid any nation which abides by the United Nations Charter and all Covenants *when it is nationally or physically abused, threatened, or attacked by another.* The attacking nation must face opposition from all other 193 (at present) united nations. *That* should give pause about even considering international aggression. United Nations Charter Articles 41 and 42 speak to this.

This does not mean that war begins. Support for the unjustly attacked nation can come in many forms. For instance, if a nation considering such an attack realized that should its attack commence: all of its assets held outside its borders would be frozen; that its borders would be closed; that its harbors and airports would be blocked, nothing would come in or go out; that its communications systems would be closed down; etc.; would that nation still carry out an attack? If it did, then that aggressor, clearly violating its signed obligations under the United Nations Charter, will be penalized, shall pay the UN Multinational Force costs and reparations; and likely experience an enforced remedial governance change by the UN *toward a peoples'* democracy. Their weapons lost in warfare will not be allowed to be replaced, a step which should cause great hesitation about even considering armed aggression.

Boulder 1: Peace in the Holy Land? What an Absurd Idea!

To many Americans the thought that Israelis and Palestinians could walk the same streets and not be constantly at each other's' throats is *absurd*. It makes about as much sense to think that, after those years of capture, and slavery in the United States, whites and blacks in America could live peacefully together. It makes about as much sense to think, after the brutality of the Pacific War, that after the nuclear inferno taking well more than 210,000 lives in Hiroshima and Nagasaki, that Americans and Japanese could ever engage in peaceful social and economic intercourse. Palestinians and Israelis cooperating and working together makes about as much sense as Japanese and Chinese economically cooperating after the murderous Asian War. <u>Absurd!</u>

In the land of Abraham and his son, Ishmael, there is *only one real, just, and fair solution* to the problems faced by the DNA-connected Palestinians and Israelis. In 1947 the United Nations General Assembly Resolution 181 established boundaries for Jewish and Arab states in the UK Palestine Mandate, **a very questionable action.** The Jews accepted; well certainly they would; the Arabs did not, *Certainly!* For some history I suggest:

https://www.aljazeera.com/news/2023/10/9/whats-the-israel-palestine-conflict-about-a-simple-guide (Palestine emerged in the 12th-century BC. There was a Jewish presence as early as 3,000 BC.) In 1948 the Palestinians and other Arabs had to make room; a great many became refugees on their own land, with little aid from the Israelis who were moving in on them. Little or no attempt was made to integrate all into a mixed society with all working to develop the land as their God might have wished. Both sides need to decide what is more important, people and society, or dirt and sand. The extremists argue incessantly, getting nowhere, while blood spills daily from the young, especially the young.

A new concept of sovereignty is required. The solution we propose is to give Palestinians their nation— in the following manner— while taking nothing away from Israel. It is a solution so absurd that it tops the list of the Ten Most Absurd Ideas.

In this absurd and moral solution Israelis would be able to build homes and settlements throughout the land; *so would Palestinians*; from Lebanon to Egypt, from the Mediterranean to Jordan and Syria. *"Parallel" Nations without separation! Nations superimposed.* The boundaries of present Israel would become also the boundaries of a Palestine. Elsewhere in the world multiethnic, multi-religious societies, intimately aware of each other, successfully live in peace. The only possible, fair, and just solution is to unify the Holy Land. Let the Israelis call it Israel. Let the Palestinians call it Palestine. *A new concept of sovereignty!* The true essence of a nation is made of people and their society, not dirt. Other mixed societies live together in peace. Maybe it is not possible for Palestinians and Israelis, who have much in common, but may be incapable of such human behavior, even though they both have a "Do onto others" equivalent admonition. An artificial intelligence search suggests that the following have successful multicultural societies: Singapore, Switzerland, Rwanda, Bolivia, Canada, Brazil, India, South Africa, New Zealand, and Malaysia. But peace and ethnic harmony are relative concepts, and even these exemplary nations face internal challenges and ongoing efforts to strengthen social cohesion, *but they do not kill one another because of disagreements.* Studying their successes and ongoing development can offer valuable insights for other societies striving to build inclusive and peaceful multicultural communities.

Imagine how successful the unified nations <u>could</u> be. Wealth now wasted on military needs of the nations would be redirected into internal developments: industry, agriculture, health needs, new housing, new schools, transportation, good water resources, and roads; the entire infrastructure. There could be carefully chosen consultants, experts, and UN advisors helping create the plans *and the support*. Outside resources could be poured into new Palestinian developments without fear that they would be bulldozed or bombed next year. Millions of people throughout the world want to visit a peaceful historical Holy Land. With the Mediterranean coast, the two nations at peace could become a holy paradise for visitors from the wide world. With Palestinian and Israeli human resources available the region could quickly become a modern progressive showplace on the sea, much like Japan became after 1945. But here the change might take place even faster because in contrast to the Japan of post-1945 there has not been as much great social and physical destruction as in the nuked cities of deadly radioactive ashes. But in 2024 Gaza seems headed that way.

Incidentally, this approach ends violent conflict between Israel and Palestine. If both peoples inhabit the entire "Israeli region" any attack or bombing by either would be an offense against themselves. And the two, united and unified, would form a greater defense against <u>hostile</u> neighbors.

But Palestinians and Israelis seem to lack something that keeps them from peaceful relationships. Other nations with histories of mortal combat are now friendly with each other. Some would quite justly claim that what is lacking here is a truly democratic Palestine, because true democracies don't typically go to war with one another, (not that Israel is a completely true democracy). But of course Palestine could not be a democracy if a Palestinian nation doesn't exist. If it did exist it might choose to form its own version of democracy. That may be a problem; nations of that region seem to be noted more for theocracy rather than for democracy; and that could be only one step away from autocracy and dictatorship. Although, if Palestinians democratically chose theocracy they could cope with that provided that they also have the power to alter the theocratic influence in their society, as is done by many people living in democracies.

As the situation stands, *nations that value* coercive indoctrination, dirt and monument preservation over fellow humans will only lead to another century or three of killing and destruction until nothing remains. Not a good prospect.

A miss-guided suicide-death for your nation is useless; you must live for your nation, work for its success. That can't be done from the grave. Just think what all of the war-disabled and war-dead of Palestine, Israel, Iraq, Iran, Afghanistan, Ukraine, Pakistan, Russia, Japan, United States, United Kingdom have lost forever.

Of the conflict in the Holy Land blame can be distributed throughout the world, including Islam. As a Pakistani scientist wrote, "For Muslims, it is time to stop wallowing in self-pity; Muslims are not helpless victims of conspiracies hatched by an all-powerful, malicious West. The fact is that the decline of Islamic greatness took place long before the age of mercantile imperialism. The causes were essentially internal. Therefore, Muslims must introspect and ask what went wrong." (Pervez Amir Ali Hoodbhoy, Washington Post, Sunday, December 30, 2001; Page B04) (One person's opinion.)

There is only one fair, just, moral, and bless'ed solution. We hope the reader will consider: whether Israelis and Palestinians would be able to live peacefully with this solution. Acceptance and acting upon it could establish Palestine and Israel as perhaps the most praiseworthy nations of the 21ˢᵗ century. **I wonder which nation may be too theocratically and mythologically tradition-trapped to be able to recognize this truth, this opportunity, to turn the deadly chaos into a new era of peace for all. Perhaps both.** Or is it just politics grinding out another continuing deadly debacle?

You may think, "Here are reasons it would not work." I will think, "Here are ways it can be made to work." It is questionable whether Israelis and Palestinians have the wisdom and patience needed for creating ways to make it work. **You are begged to consider the problems that will arise and exist for a _separate_ Palestinian nation, problems that will continue to prevent peace throughout the _Eastern Mediterranean/Middle East (EMME)_. Acceptance and working out this solution would only result in greater social wealth and peace for all.**

This absurd concept of sovereignty seems to be the only one capable of making the 21ˢᵗ Century in the Holy Land as radiant as was intended. Albert Einstein observed, "If at first the idea is not absurd, then there is no hope for it." Maybe that's a good sign. Obviously, this is an attempt to correct the UN-UK errors made in 1947. **Einstein, at age 73, while supportive of Israel, preferred a binational Jewish-Arab state over a separate Jewish state.**

The world has seen enough of artificially newly formed nations in the past-century to realize that such paths are disastrous: Vietnam, Korea, Pakistan, Yugoslavia, Kashmir, Ethiopia, Sudan, Soviet Union, Cyprus, Somalia. . . . A nation to be based on a specific religion, one could easily anticipate the troubles to be. I believe there are many Israelis and Palestinians, _living in EMME lands and throughout the world_, who would see _this_ two-state unification as _a difficult but proper moral solution_ to the problem.

Worldwide in 2024 there are an estimated 130 million refugees now in camps, or forcibly displaced globally, or wandering the earth hoping that somewhere they can find a peaceful existence. Maybe the UN should again establish Mandates that could accommodate _these_ displaced souls. _Surely_, on this earth there must be some nations, states, and regions willing to move around and make space for these nationless people, perhaps like the U.S. did, *for some*, in the early 1900s. There are some American states that still have low population densities like: Montana, Vermont, South and North Dakota, Wyoming, Nebraska, Louisiana, etc. *Surely there is a place for the 130 million, somewhere.* God bless them. The United Nations General Assembly Resolution 181 of 1947 literally created Palestinian refugees, a very questionable act. It is possible that Israel, the UN, and Palestinians may never find peace until they take note of and use Einstein's admonition, "We can't solve problems by using the same kind of thinking we used when we created them." **One can easily understand the impact that this "Incentivization" program could have for a Bi-National Jewish-Arab State. No more war, $2 Billion per year for social development for 25 years affecting both nations. Surely no preference to kill and destroy.**

Boulder 2: National Tendencies toward Imperialism

Michael Parenti [16]: "…empires are not innocent, absent-minded, accidental accretions. They are given purposive direction by rulers who consciously mobilize vast amounts of personnel and materials in order to plunder other lands and peoples."

The Germans did not occupy France just for the wine, women, and art. The Japanese did not just happen to find themselves in Manchuria. The U.S. has some 700 or more military bases *in at least 70 countries and territories (2024).*

Parenti, again: "The Americans did not just mistakenly stumble into Iraq…Imperialism is what empires do…. The intervention [of imperialism] is intended to *enrich the investors* and *keep the world safe for them.* … In addition to the pillage of their lands,…[Empires] impoverish whole populations and slaughter huge numbers of innocent people. …**Do those who preside over the U.S. empire believe in their own virtue?...But even more so, more than anything else in the world, with the utmost dedication and ferocity, *they believe in protecting and advancing their own material interests…they do whatever it takes to do so.*"**

If it looks like an empire, acts like an empire, and maliciously plunders like an empire, then it probably is an empire.

In contrast to the multitude of opaque secrets, corruptions, overt and covert illegal actions *this proposed workable moral strategy, The Incentivization of World Peace,* would renew the faith of many Americans and the world that the United States was not imperialistic. Who wants to be Emperor?

However, "The powers of financial capitalism had a far-reaching [plan], nothing less than to create a world system of financial control *in private hands* able to dominate the political system of each country and the economy of the world as a whole." —Carroll Quigley, author of Tragedy and Hope: A History of the World in Our Time, **1359 pages**, [5] An abbreviated account of those 1359 pages can be read in, W. Cleon Skousen's THE NAKED CAPITALIST [17]. It is a review, considered a right-wing review by some, with commentary. You may also wish to check what Wikipedia has to say about W. Cleon Skousen, and also the single-star Reviews of Skousen's book on Amazon.com.

Einstein wrote, "The result of these developments is an oligarchy of *private* capital the enormous power of which cannot be effectively checked even by a democratically organized political society. This is true since the members of legislative bodies are selected by political parties, largely financed or otherwise influenced by *private* capitalists who, for all practical purposes, separate the electorate from the legislature. *The consequence is that the representatives of the people do not in fact sufficiently protect the interests of the underprivileged sections of the population.* Moreover, under existing conditions, *private* capitalists inevitably control, directly or indirectly, the main sources of information (press, radio, education). It is thus extremely difficult, and indeed in most cases quite impossible, for the individual citizen to come to objective conclusions and to make intelligent use of his political rights..."

"...This *crippling of individuals* I consider the worst evil of capitalism. Our whole educational system suffers from this evil. *An exaggerated competitive attitude is inculcated into the student, who is trained to worship acquisitive success as a preparation for his future career.*"

"...how is it possible, in view of the far-reaching centralization of political and economic power, to prevent bureaucracy from becoming all-powerful and overweening? *How can the rights of the individual be protected and therewith a democratic counterweight to the power of bureaucracy be assured?*" [italics by R.W.] —Albert Einstein, *"Why Socialism?,"* first issue of Monthly Review (May 1949) The reader is strongly encouraged to consider Einstein's entire somewhat brief commentary which he concluded with that question. The article is available online at, http://monthlyreview.org/2009/05/01/why-socialism

Boulder 3.
Extraterritorial Claims

These three fictional nations share common borders with each other. It has been determined that in this region there is a very rich underground deposit of natural gas and oil, the field extending beneath all three nations and probably into the waters outside their borders. This is a natural resource that all three nations have in common. A more important natural resource are the people of these nations. So far no nation has tapped this resource and there is some fear that when one nation begins extraction the entire wealth will accrue to that nation alone. Shall the wealth go

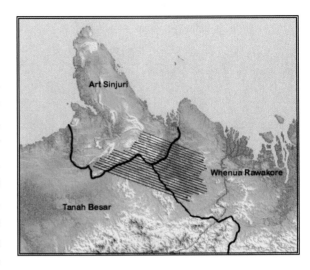

to first come, first served? Will a wealthy outside nation step in and offer to quickly set up high capacity pumping wells and ship this crude product abroad for processing? Can this situation become a conflict leading to war among the three nations, sacrificing the human resource because of the material one? Would two nations cooperate to repel the third nation's efforts to hog it all? What would be fair? As an outsider, what would you recommend?

In 2014 it was easy to understand the extraterritorial claims of nations in Asia. There are proven oil resources in the offshore waters and exploration continues for more oil as the energy needs of Asian nations expand. Taiwan and Japan have very limited natural reserves of oil. China, at one time, was an oil exporter; it is now (2024) the world's largest importer of oil while strongly relying on its coal resources to fuel its energy industry, a very polluting

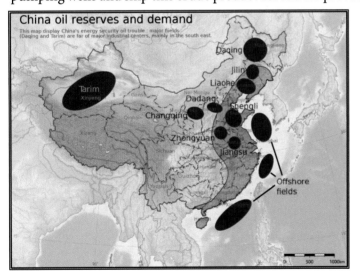

Oil map of China. Author, East_Asia_topographic_map.png: Ksiom (derivative work: Yug)

approach, but one which all industrial nations have experienced in the last 100-200 years.

The waters off the coast of China where oil is found have become regions of dispute. Claims have been made over off-mainland island territories that have been administered by one nation or another for more than 100 years; administration usually beginning after a military conflict, e.g., the almost 80 year Russian administration of the Kuril Islands north of Hokkaido.

In May, 1969 a UN report suggested that there may be oil deposits in the region of the Senkaku Islands, known in China as the Diaoyu Islands, and known in Taiwan as the Diaoyutai Islands; hence as one might expect, a dispute arises about which nation holds true sovereignty. It is a very messy problem as this Wikipedia page illustrates. Internet search: **wikipedia, Senkaku Islands dispute**

Further elucidation is here,
https://www.tofugu.com/japan/senkaku-islands/

Author: Jackopoid

It is not likely that this sovereignty question will be solved based upon historical precedents. What should then be expected? Will the wisdom of the orient use <u>new ways of thinking</u> in order to resolve this problem without sacrificing human resources?

Do these three nations realize how strongly they are dependent upon one another? This is how capitalistic competition brings nations to conflict and sometimes to war. It is likely that this competition-to-conflict is what Asian nations have learned from the West. We now have a chance to see whether the wisdom of the Orient will achieve something better than militarized industrial complexes of western "Christian, developed nations" could manage. Here is a possibility toward an actual tri-prosperity venture, a venture wherein everyone benefits and no one is war-sacrificed. Should we, can we expect something better from these three nations?

Taiwan, Japan, and China, all at the present time (2024) make use of one another's resources, both natural and human. All have entered into joint ventures with one another. Why not consider here a *joint venture in exploration and utilization of the possible resources to be found in this area of the East China Sea*. Eventually, *depletion* is going to force attempts to capture and utilize such natural resources. Why not do it peacefully for everyone's benefit without resorting to, as Eisenhower put it, "stupid war". What shall be put into practice, wisdom or stupidity?

In this current problem Senkaku would be the responsibility of Japan to lead toward a solution. Administration of that area has been theirs for some 129 years. Are there any Japanese government officials who can be guided by the highest social morals and ethics to have the foresight and courage to see a brilliant, intelligent, and peaceful resolution, or shall we all by hindsight witness more destruction and death brought about by a "stupid war" of greed for oil.

How would the world's people view a cooperative peaceful solution?

Boulder 4:
International Financial Corruption (Too large a topic to be covered here)
Boulders 5, 6,… (To be provided by the reader)

Developing nations, yielding their military burden in favor of democracy, (social democracy?), and peaceful progress, must have assurances that they will be *quickly and adequately protected*, not necessarily with military force, by the UN and the strongest powers of the world. North Korea, Iran, Israel, the U.S, and other nations need to understand what changes they need to make to receive assurances and protection against attack by any other nation. "Minds more wise," not pre-programmed bureaucrats nor dysfunctional politicians, must speak to United Nations Charter revisions. Because all nations are not equal there should be special rules to apply to emerging, developing nations for the protection of their people from corrupt governance and from powerful outside political and exploitive influences.

We ask the reader to actually consider what would result should this workable Incentivization of World Peace be offered to the United Nations, and further what would result if the membership of the United Nations agreed to its implementation. Can you imagine the absurd arguments against it, Two Billion Dollars yearly for Developing Nations, and a world at peace?

Summary II

Greater security for all nations can be obtained by *worldwide reduction* of the weapons of all nations rather than increasing and improving arsenals everywhere, as we are doing, and as has been done for past centuries. You see the results. **The next <u>world nuclear war</u> will kill more people than all the wars preceding it; I'm fairly sure, and AI-Gemini agrees.**

Nations which truly abide by the intentions of the United Nations Charter pose no malicious economic, territorial, or military threats to their neighbors. *Is that not what signatures on the UN Charter imply?* Implementing this workable moral strategy will have more than US$330 billion each year eliminating military and economic threats, while peace and justice advance throughout the world, ***the mother of all great bargains***.

This proposal is probably the only approach, for decades or centuries to come, by which people of the Less developed world, in peace, can become their own masters, can create the sensible path to their own destinies as so many other nations have. This is *not a threat* to the Developed world. Peace with fairness, justice, and international cooperation, is preferable to war, anytime.

When nations and regions are at peace, helping one another, they advance! It is obvious! It is not by mere coincidence that the nation of Japan, after its near total war-time destruction, has since 1945 made astonishing advances in all aspects of human activity without killing anyone in a war. China has shown remarkable advancements in living and working conditions and great accomplishments in their infrastructure, though the early days were questionable. India and Pakistan, Iraq and Iran, could do the same. But how will they manage if a world economic downturn prevents and stops financial aid?

Perhaps India, Pakistan, and Bangladesh should never have been separated. Was there no other way? Had they been able to live peacefully together imagine the advances that would have been possible. Bangladesh and Pakistan might have become part of the advances now moving through India; there could likely have been no battles and skirmishes along the border with Afghanistan—everyone would have been too busy on the job, building better homes, attending school, improving their lives (problems related to the Durand Line (western border)). Now there is the prospect of a nuclear confrontation; they could stupidly destroy themselves. Before the separation would life in India have been different if every child of India had been well-fed and well-educated? Before the separation—every child!

Should there be any doubts in the minds of people of the earth as to the desires of the United States for world peace with justice and fairness for all nations, presentation of this workable moral strategy by the United States government to the world's nations would put such doubts to rest. For the foreseeable future, it is the responsibility of the United States to guide the world in the direction of world peace; no other nation will; no other nation can. This superpower, capable of destroying the world, is apparently the only one, at present, with the capability, dependent upon the concepts of freedom, fairness, and justice, to move the world to peace. Do it while not seeking personal advantage.

For the naysayers who would claim it cannot be done, such massive programs have in the past been carried out somewhat successfully. The Marshall Plan (1948) is an example, the Molotov Plan (1947) is another, as are Post-Soviet Aid (1991) and USAID programs. ***This proposed moral strategy has even greater potential, can involve 196 nations and <u>it has safeguards against abuse and corruption.</u>***

In 2024 industrialized nations are racing to courtship with African nations that have natural resources of fossil fuels, rare metals, and people. This is all to the good and one can be thankful that African nations will not be as naïve as they were in past decades or centuries; advantage of them will likely not be taken. However, in this modern age of *private* investments in Less Developed nations there is always the likelihood of corruption. Some of the projects will greatly help the advancement of some African people, but there are signs of potential conflict. Small farmers of Mozambique fear that their agricultural lands will be taken over by large multinational corporations in the name of economic growth. Egypt fears for its water supply as Ethiopia builds a giant dam, the Grand Ethiopian Renaissance Dam (GERD) on the Nile River that will create a reservoir of 74 million cubic meters of water. Kenyan legislators recently voted to keep their lavish salaries; the Kenyan President's salary is more than 200 times the minimum Kenyan wage of about $1500 per year, and some earn less. Where does the money come from? Possibly investment from outside interests? **Our *workable moral strategy* would safeguard workers in Less Developed nations from such exploitation.**

Among the nations pursuing new goals in Africa are: Japan, China, India, South Korea, and undoubtedly all other large industrialized nations. Japan's 2014 then Prime Minister Abe has said Japan will pledge up to 3.2 trillion Yen (US$32 billion) in *government* and *private* aid for five years; will spend 650 billion Yen (US$4.0 billion) on African infrastructure; will educate and train 31,000 African youth to help them get jobs; will promote "universal" basic health services in Africa; and will seek to transition Africa's agricultural systems to one in which farmers can earn money as well as feed themselves. Two major Japanese goals will be rural electrification and the development of "international corridors" that will link the African interior with the African coast. These two items would facilitate extraction of natural resources from the interior and enable shipment to friends abroad. Then Prime Minister Abe has said to the African nations, use the aid as you see fit. Oh-oh! (The Japan Times, June 2, 2013) These seem to be admirable goals but are there any guarantees against abuse and corruption? After all, the money comes from Japanese labor. In the same edition of The Japan Times, Jeff Kingston wrote, "Crony capitalism is the scourge of contemporary Asia, lining pockets and diverting resources in ways that systematically undermine the public interest, accentuate disparities, sap innovative and entrepreneurial impulses—while also subverting governance." Kingston added that in Transparency International's 2012 Corruption Index of 174 nations and territories, Scores: (0-100; 0 = highly corrupt; 100 = clean) China and India rank 39 and 36 respectively, which means both are considered highly corrupt. Russia was 28. Japan ranked 74, the U.S., 73. The 2023 list is here: **https://www.transparency.org/en/cpi/2023/index/aus**. In 2023 we have China, 42, India, 39, Japan, 73, U.S., 69, Russia,26,out of 180 countries and territories.)

Is there anything really surprising here? For centuries now, rich nations have found ways to exploit poor nations, and often try to make it appear that they have the highest human and moral goals in doing so. But, examined more closely, among humanity, morality, and politics, the rich nations will usually place politics first, with the hope that humanity will somehow, if possible, be aided in a moral manner.

James C. Warf,
1993, Indonesia

Albert Einstein wrote, "…unless by common struggle we are capable of *new ways of thinking*, mankind is doomed." At present we are bound by political thinking, much of which seems dictated by private financial interests, not human or necessarily moral interests. The late James C. Warf, former Manhattan Project plutonium scientist and USC distinguished professor of chemistry, realized that the ideas expressed in this workable moral strategy represented a useful *new way of thinking* about achieving and preserving peace. Warf incorporated an early form of this workable moral strategy into his excellent 2005 book, *All Things Nuclear*. [18] It is a splendid work that reads at times like a novel.

Barack Obama pro-claimed, "For unlike the great powers of old, we have not sought world domination. Our union was founded in resistance to oppression. We do not seek to occupy other nations. We will not claim another nation's resources or target other peoples because their faith or ethnicity is different from ours." (His speech at West Point, Dec. 1, 2009)

President Obama did not exclude "protecting our vital interests" in other nations, claiming access to resources and targeting *for other reasons*. If given half a chance, other nations can protect their own vital interests. That sounds like Russia "protecting its vital interests" in the Crimea and Ukraine; Russia certainly has vital interests there, Russian people (lots of them), its Black Sea fleet, history. It is another mess. I'm writing in November, 2024. Will Ukraine and Crimea become Russian, again?

This workable moral strategy derived from **Oppenheimer's 1946 Conjecture** and Einstein's and Shohno's writings are sometimes criticized as being too futuristic and difficult to implement. But there are no *technical* implementation difficulties, only those difficulties of critical thinking in people's minds. The necessary wiser minds must be found. Many hoped that Barack Obama was sufficiently wise to do it. Many did not foresee the obstructions to a peaceful world that he would face. Biden has faced greater obstruction which is even nonsensical and political stupidity. In 2025 we will see something different.

Yes, wars are much easier to implement. Simpletons and madmen can get them going. The United States is all set up for them now. We are not, however, set up to implement world peace. In 1917 and again in 1941 the U.S. did not have enough money or gold; but resources, men and material, and women, we did have. Those resources made it possible for us to achieve the high production and efficiency required to end those wars. Unfortunately we only do this when **going to war**. Our sin of active complacency and poor congressional leadership and cooperation prevents us from engaging in the much more rewarding struggle of **going to peace**.

Changes in Our "Developed" World

Each year this workable moral strategy would see returned to the nonmilitary economies of the Developed nations, in total, more than US $330 billion, creating well more than 1,000,000 jobs worldwide, mostly manufacturing and construction! It is money most of which ordinarily would have been spent for non-wealth-creating new military weapons and systems. It has been remarked that, "…non-military spending can create more jobs than money going to defense programs." Research by the Costs of War Project indicates that education, particularly elementary and secondary education, creates significantly more jobs per dollar spent compared to the military sector. In their findings, every $1 million invested in education creates nearly three times as many jobs as the same amount spent on defense. [AI – Gemini] **The proposed strategy should greatly reduce unemployment in any nation adopting it.**

With nations in full peacetime production and without threats of war, national debts should be payable. Workers with money in their pockets would stimulate other domestic industries which would not be dependent upon the chit payouts. New ventures in energy production, medical instrumentation, nano electronics, transportation, communications, etc., could proceed without chit payout funds. What effect would a thriving well-managed economy have on social problems? Would it make them solvable? If the economies and opportunities in Central American nations were thriving, would Latinos still wish to migrate to America for maybe immediate menial jobs?

This workable moral strategy implies that an exchange could be made:

- ☯ With self-sufficiency and self-defined but true democracy in the developing world and the virtual elimination there of poverty, illiteracy, malnutrition, disease, neocolonialism, rights deprivation, indebtedness, exploitation, and slavery;
- ☯ The entire world could have full economic recovery, elimination of the possibility for international nuclear catastrophe, and the practical elimination of war. In a world at peace the refugee problem is solved. The killing stops and solutions to *worldwide* problems can be sought and found.

The basic tool is incentives, not sanctions; benefits, not penalties; advantages for all as the wise men knew it could be. **If you prefer NOT destroying all weapons of war, then disable them and put them under UN-Guaranteed Lock and Key?**

A World of Opportunities

Most impoverished nations, at present, do not have the capability to fully utilize all their arable land and create more. Implementation of this moral strategy would change that. With help from the United Nations and organizations like the semi-governmental JICA (Japan International Cooperation Agency) appropriate agriculture can squeeze the maximum benefits annually out of lands considered not fruitful. Ichiro Kawasaki in his 1955 book, *The Japanese Are Like That*, [19] remarked that, the entire nation of Japan, population, 126.5 million (2024), has always had less good farm land than all of the mountainous state of Kentucky. And yes, we do recognize that unlike Kentucky Japan does have the Pacific Ocean also as an additional food source. The oceans and seas are "free", and accessible to many Less Developed nations.

Some less advantaged nations find themselves in dry climates, hindering agriculture. Potential agricultural areas of India are dry and dusty. India, Pakistan, and Bangladesh could benefit from better control and utilization of monsoon waters and Himalayan runoff. That could be altered; deserts can bloom. It was once seriously proposed that the dry plains of the middle United States and Canada could be fed by *fresh* water desalinized from Hudson Bay. What would Canada charge the U.S. for that fresh water? International foresight and cooperation could make such projects feasible and beneficial. More water desalinization and purification projects in the Middle East, Africa, and Australia could greatly improve living, health, and economic conditions in those areas. It could open up new territories for presently huddled masses. How many people would desalinization projects employ?

Appropriate energy technology can serve the needs of developing nations. Fortunately many such nations are in areas where winter heating needs may be small. Until recently Japanese homes had minimal heating: a *kotatsu* table or space heater. On the African continent hydroelectric power and solar electricity are developing energy sources, especially solar. The indigenous people supply the labor at a good salary building and maintaining the system; the developed world supplies the knowledge, teaching, generators, and technology. Rural electrification can do wonders for country people.

The energy produced by nuclear reactions can be one hundred thousand to one million times greater than the energy produced by the most energetic chemical reactions (burning). Consider the extremes to which the world goes in order to extract fossil fuels from the earth, "fracking," deep ocean drilling, horizontal drilling beneath national borders, bituminous sands, war for control of "vital interests," etc.; eventually there will be no more nature-created fossil fuels. In this energy-gobbling century #21, when we know there are dwindling reservoirs of nature-stored energy, would it not be foolish to ignore the safe use of nuclear-generated energy? How could a Less Developed nation compete with ExxonMobil, Total S.A., British Petroleum, Chevron, ConocoPhillips, and Royal Dutch Shell, if it wants to become part of the developed world?

Access to energy is a key to economic development in impoverished parts of the world; sustainable energy fosters enterprise activities that break the cycle of poverty. In 2012 the United Nations, estimated that 1.4 billion people did not have access to electricity; declared the year 2012 to be the International Year of Sustainable Energy for All. In 2024 that number has been reduced to about 775,000 people. (AI-Gemini).

Nuclear power should not be overlooked; there are safe power reactors that could be placed over safe geology. The "hub-spoke" arrangement [19], sometimes called "nuclear batteries," ("*Batteries Included,*" Bulletin of the Atomic Scientists, Nov/Dec, 2006, p. 19) holds promise and would seem to be a very sensible way for developing nations to quickly meet energy needs, *if there are no other possible resources.* Radioactive waste remains a solvable problem; at present, this writer's preference is for nuclear incineration to much shorter half-lives. With IAEA oversight reprocessing and renewing spent fuel elements need not be a problem. We are aware of strong objections to this, and we have learned much from Fukushima, Chernobyl, Three-Mile Island, and elsewhere. How much more of the earth can we risk with radioactive contamination? **Non-nuclear would be better.** In 2012 of the fifty Japanese nuclear power plants only two units of the Oi plant were in operation; many in Japan would like both units also shut down. What stress does this place on world energy sources?

Critical comments follow the SA article. In 2014 Japan's Prime Minister supported nuclear energy for Japan. In 2022 of 33 operable plants, 10 were in operation in Japan.

Better yet would be, where appropriate, solar or wind generation and storage of electricity. Energy storage is a rapidly evolving field, and new technologies are constantly being developed. A good career prospect?

Perhaps the greatest danger in this workable moral strategy might be the personal avarice of those participating, just as it has been in nations for centuries, dangerous among nations and industries. This workable moral strategy will need to set in place procedures to guard against such dangers.

Shortly after WWII Truman was told that if he expected American taxpayers to finance a military buildup in the aftermath of the war's sacrifices he would have to "scare the hell out of them." A very good job was done, continuing to the present day.

But Eisenhower warned us in his farewell message, "America's leadership [in the world] depends, not merely upon our unmatched material progress, riches and military strength, but on how we use our power in the interests of world peace and human betterment..." "...we have been **compelled** to create a permanent armaments industry of vast proportions..." "...We annually spend on military security more than the net income of all United States corporations..."

We need to examine the origins of that **compulsion**. Does it still exist, and if so, why? What, or who, has prevented ending the compulsion? Internal or external influences; Russia or China or war mongers?
Eisenhower saw what was coming, "… In the councils of government, we must guard against the acquisition of unwarranted influence, *whether sought or unsought*, by the military-industrial complex. The potential for the disastrous rise of displaced power exists and will persist. We must never let the weight of this combination endanger our liberties or democratic processes." In the U.S. Lockheed Martin is the largest manufacturer and supplier of military weapons.
Should the U.S. go to war to protect **"our vital interests abroad"**? The meaning of "to protect" has been essentially "to secure and control." In the early 1900's the Japanese government did not bother to ask their people just as our government has not asked us for our approval of going to war for such reasons. After the Russo-Japanese war (1904-1905) Japan found itself occupying much of Manchuria and after the Russian

Revolution of 1917 Japan exerted even greater influence in Manchuria, taking advantage, beyond its borders, "to secure and control" and hence "to protect" "its vital resources" of coal, iron ore and other minerals, and the soil for its soy and barley production. Has the United States itself been "occupying" other nations? How can one nation claim "its vital resources" when they are in another nation?

It is said that Japan might not have been able to wage war in Asia if it did not have the raw materials of Manchuria, their (Japan's) "vital resources." Where did Japan get those vital resources that were necessary for their economic miracle <u>after</u> 1945? And without war? From newly found friends. Perhaps the U.S. is afraid that it would not be able to conduct war if it loses access to its "vital resources" in the Middle East. Where would the U.S. get those vital resources after 2024? Without war? It could get them from newly found friends.

"It is not an exaggeration to say that it is clearly in the interests of the world's leading arms exporters to make sure that there is always a war going on somewhere." (Marilyn Waring, Documentary, *'Who's Counting'*, based on her book, *Counting for Nothing*, University of Toronto Press, 1999. [21]

But if there were no wars to be fought, what would be the fate and future of the arms makers and exporters? If they wanted to stay in business they would be beating those swords and spears into plowshares, pruning hooks, infrastructures and exporting them to those who need them.

Justification: A Moral World View

Do the people of the Developed World have any responsibility for the conditions of poverty, starvation, slavery, disease, displaced refugees, rights deprivation, war and killing, and illiteracy, etc., as they now exist in the former colonial and Less Developed world, in Africa, in Asia and the Middle East, in Latin America? Your answer might depend in part on whether you and your nation have taken selfish advantage of those people. Over past centuries has the Developed World exploited the people of the UnDeveloped World? If so, does the Developed World have any unfulfilled moral obligations to the former colonial world?

Many believe it does. I have always thought—I was taught—that the United States and other Developed nations considered themselves to be moral nations, whether Christian or not. Whether or not you agree, the past 80 years of Developed World taxation for military purposes, in deterrent preparation for a possible Nuclear WWIII holocaust, clearly shows that, *if the developed world is not militarily or significantly economically threatened*, then it can afford to meet "moral obligations" to the less developed world. **The moral strategy is for US$330 billion per year for 20 to 25 years to meet this obligation,** while simultaneously ending wars and alleviating international hostilities, conflicts, and the need for war armaments, **via the originally stated specifications of this workable moral strategy**. It is not expected that international or national conflicts will vanish, but there would be procedures in place, early, for rectification without resort to murder on the large scale. Wiser minds, which we must find, can see to that. There have been some in the past, but people do not always listen. "I believe that all men are my brothers . . . tolerance and kindness can overcome differences in race, culture and language." —James A. Michener

The $330 billion carries with it a bonus. Since it supplies the tools needed for developing a nation, they do not get used up after the first year, as money does. They continue usage which multiplies as more tools and knowledge are added in the following years until, after 20 years or so there can be a nation fully equipped with the tools needed for continued advancement. WOW! What a bargain!

It seems that the U.S. governing body in 2020-2024 thinks that they have matters of greater importance with which to deal. Do we need wiser minds in government?

Some will say that war is part of human nature and can't be avoided. Nonsense! The United States and Canada will not go to war. Truly democratic nations will not go to war; will not even prepare for war with each other. Spencer Weart has written about this in his book, *Never At War: Why Democracies Will Not Fight One Another* [22]. (Of course, over the past 200 years how many truly democratic nations have there been? Well, even if the idea is only 96% true, that's pretty damn good.)

Elimination of the tools of war: There need be no problem with verification or with guarded conversion of fissionable nuclear material and the chemical, biological and other tools of war; these are solvable human problems, and not problems of technology. *Mankind can make all nuclear weapons unusable easily within a few years if there is a genuine will and need to do so.* Apparently Russia was willing to trust the U.S. to do so in the offers presented at the Reagan-Gorbachev Summit in Iceland in 1986. Mr. Putin may not agree in 2024.

From the catastrophes at Hiroshima and Nagasaki some of us have learned it is most imperative that the world verifiably rid itself of all nuclear weapons. Though some nuclear disarming has been underway there still remain the real fears concerning: proliferation, Reliable Replacement Warheads (RRW), nuclear breakouts and terrorism, and our "new enemies." The danger continues, as Oppenheimer in 1946 recognized it would; "nuclear weapons can be very effective." There still remain in this third decade of the 21st century some 12,600 nuclear warheads.[FAS] It was once said that 300 might be a sufficient deterrent. If there were none…?

This workable moral strategy represents one certain way for the elimination of international war for all people of the Earth. It is also probably the *only* method, for decades or centuries to come, by which people of the Less Developed world, in peace, can become their own masters, can create the sensible path to their own destinies as so many other nations have. This strategy is not a threat to the Developed World. Peace with justice and fairness is preferable to war, anytime.

For those Developing nations and those who repeatedly blame America and international capitalism for all the ills of the world and all the troubles in their nations, here is their chance to successfully move into the future without necessarily being sucked up into commitments and obligations to Developed World Powers, to the World Bank, and to the International Monetary Fund. How many leaders of Developing nations are willing to put their people first, rather than their military? How many will build schools and hospitals, homes and farms, rather than nuclear fortresses, glorious palaces, and monuments? Which leaders of the Developed AND Developing nations will become immortalized as the ones who led their nation to the "New World," rather than as the ones who kept them chained to a past of perpetual wars and misery? When will they awaken to a "new way of thinking"? Is time running out? Have we waited too long? **Francis Bacon observed, "He that will not apply new remedies must expect new evils; for time is the greatest innovator."**

There can be a peaceful world with justice and fairness for all if both Developed and Developing nations have the hindsight, foresight and courage, to view the world, to think about the world, in new ways. The most effective use of military *budgets* is, not resorting to murderous war, but the *proactive* conversion of extant or potential enemies into equal and cooperative friends, all working for a peaceful world with justice and fairness for all people and all nations. **Can you conceive of a better way for a nation's military budget to protect its citizens? This workable moral strategy shows how such a world at peace can be achieved. So if we send the military on a mission which is really the responsibility of the Executive Department, <u>that would be proper use of the military budget</u>. We are on the right path!**

"The day will come when the progress of nations will be judged not by their military or economic strength, nor by the splendor of their capital cities and public buildings, but by the well-being of their people: by their levels of health, nutrition and education; by their opportunities to earn a fair reward for their labors; by their ability to participate in the decisions that affect their lives; by the respect that is shown for their civil and political liberties; by the provision that is made for those who are vulnerable and disadvantaged; and by the protection that is afforded to the growing minds and bodies of their children." —Peter Adamson of UNICEF (Preamble to the Progress of Nations Report 1993--following up on promises made at the 1990 World Summit for Children)

If you **do not** find yourself in agreement with this workable moral strategy for achieving and preserving world peace, then it is possible that you are not on the track set for the world in the Charter of the United Nations to which members obligated themselves with their signatures on June 26, 1945 and later. In case you have forgotten here is what members vowed to do, and to which they should be held accountable and responsible:

The Purposes of the United Nations Are: [13]

1. **To maintain international peace and security, and to that end: to take effective collective measures for the prevention and removal of threats to the peace, and for the suppression of acts of aggression or other breaches of the peace, and to bring about by peaceful means, and in conformity with the principles of justice and international law, adjustment or settlement of international disputes or situations which might lead to a breach of the peace;**
2. **To develop friendly relations among nations based on respect for the principle of equal rights and self-determination of peoples, and to take other appropriate measures to strengthen universal peace;**
3. **To achieve international cooperation in solving international problems of an economic, social, cultural, or humanitarian character, and in promoting and encouraging respect for human rights and for fundamental freedoms for all without distinction as to race, sex, language, or religion; and**
4. **To be a centre for harmonizing the actions of nations in the attainment of these common ends.**

World Peace Is Possible Now

Nowhere in this essay has World Government been proposed, but perhaps every three or five years all nations should formally renew their pledge to all the world peace and cooperation goals of the United Nations.

All people, including national leaders and legislators, should reread the first 6 articles of the United Nations Charter and *understand their nations' obligations to this world.*

The people of the world, especially people of enduring regional conflicts, plead for peace, plead for an end to the killing, torture, destruction, contamination of their lands, suffering, occupation, imprisonment, deprivation of their human and civil rights, and destruction of theirs and their children's futures. Leaders, because of greed, ideology, isolated ignorance, internal and external collusion, and misunderstood mythology, will not achieve the sought-for peace. **We have shown how it could be done.** True peace with justice and fairness is not something to be bargained for in secret or in corporate boardrooms. Try to understand what is in **The Universal Declaration of Human Rights (UDHR) adopted by the UN General Assembly in 1948.**

In **2001**, the World Bank and the United Nations have stated the reasonableness of our *workable moral strategy*: "Afghanistan needs about $9 billion during the next *five* years to rebuild after 20 years of war, the United Nations and World Bank have calculated." That is only $1.8 billion per year for five years, only 0.45% of a U.S. Annual $400++ billion Military budget (2001). And via our *workable moral strategy* half of this cost would have been contributed by all other developed nations. Why was the $9 billion not used first for the people of Afghanistan instead of destruction? By April, 2004, donors had already pledged $8.2 billion. You see how easy it might be to get the resources if it means peace. How much will be wasted or stolen by corruption and greed? And now, in 2024, I really don't know if any of the pledged funds have been used. Some Afghan regional lords were asking for about $25 billion; perhaps they were hoping to use some of the money to rearm. As I write, there are estimates that the U.S. has spent over $2 trillion in Afghanistan; what peaceful future is there in store for Afghanistan? Was $9 billion used for building a social and economic structure? What horrible mistakes were made, costing many lives! Here is world military spending; [23]. More than 120,000 lives were lost there.

Should there be any doubts in the minds of people of the earth as to the desires of the United States for world peace with justice and fairness for all nations, presentation of this *workable moral strategy* by the United States government to the United Nations would put such doubts to rest. In contrast to the multitude of secrets, corruptions, overt and covert illegal actions, this strategy would renew the faith of many Americans *and the world* that the United States was seeking world peace, was *not* pursuing imperialism.

Concerning U.S. activities and operations in the Middle East we would be wise to heed Einstein's admonition, "Henceforth *every* nation's foreign policy must be judged at every point by one consideration: does it lead us to a world of law and order or does it lead us back toward anarchy and death?" What does the world have in 2024, law and order or anarchy and death? Einstein was once offered the Presidency of Israel. What a wise man!

Gen. Butler expressed his grave concern with America's out-of-control militarism and racist imperialism in a number of articles, letters and speeches. For instance, in a 1933 speech, he declared, "War is just a racket. A racket is best described, I believe, as something that is not what it seems to the majority of people. Only a small inside group knows what it is about. It is conducted for the benefit of the very few at the expense of the masses…. The trouble with America is that when the dollar only earns 6 percent over here, then it gets restless and goes overseas to get 100 percent. Then the flag follows the dollar and the soldiers follow the flag. I wouldn't go to war again as I have done to protect some lousy investment of the bankers. There are only two things we should fight for. One is the defense of our homes and the other is the Bill of Rights. War for any other reason is simply a racket." "General Smedley Darlington Butler's Shocking Revelations of U.S. Meddling"

Internet search: **General Smedley Darlington sButler's Shocking Revelations of U.S. Meddling**

The very significant virtue of the *workable moral strategy* described here is that the dollar never goes overseas, the flag stays home, and the soldiers stay home. The currencies of all **participating nations stay home, so also, their flags and their soldiers.**

"The real truth of the matter is, as you and I know, that a financial element in the large centers has owned the government of the United States since the days of Andrew Jackson." —**Franklin D. Roosevelt [R. Wilson comment: The financial element, the owners, spending $20 Trillion on tools of death and destruction have done a lousy job. It is obvious they have conflicting interests.]**

There is considerable reason to believe President Roosevelt's statement is true, thus the "financial element in the large centers" shares responsibility and blame for the tens, if not hundreds, of thousands of war deaths in the last few decades. The people of the world need protection from those responsible for provoking nations to war. In the United States this responsibility lies with all elements in the highest levels of government, the decision makers. It lies with those who tinker with political and economic machinations, most likely for the advantage of "a financial element in the large centers." These are probably people young enough and sufficiently uninformed to have *no conception* of the atrocity of the nuclear confrontations and conflagrations to which they are quite possibly leading the world. This group of people may include most people serving in the U.S. Congress and from personal experience almost everyone in the U.S. Military. (I received no training about nuclear war while serving in the Army.) I have my doubts whether Presidents have seen all of the results of the world's first nuclear war; they are probably protected from this. Photographs of the victims were confiscated and held confidential for more than 22 years after 1945. There were well more than 210,000 victims; not many photographs were made

and survived. **You can see in this book a tiny fraction of the truth about what happens to people caught in nuclear war. In a future war there would be hundreds of thousands, more likely hundreds of millions, of victims. The United States government has not revealed this kind of truth about its first nuclear war. Obama has been the only sitting president to visit Hiroshima, with Prime Minister Abe, in 2016.**

This present document has described *a workable moral strategy* that could avoid wars and lead to a peaceful world. It is indeed a plan for the **<u>Incentivization of World Peace</u>**. It is workable; it could be done. Carried out for the world it might be considered the "ultimate kindness." What forces in the world would reject such kindness and why would they do it? Einstein evaluated every nation's foreign policy by one criterion: "Does it lead us to a world of law and order or does it lead us back toward anarchy and death?"

If you prefer NOT destroying all weapons of war, then how about, as a first step, **disabling** them and putting them under **UN-Guaranteed Lock and Key**?

AFTERWORD

Russia and the U.S. and Putin are one kind of problem. The U.S. and China is a problem of a different kind. We hear our politicians speak of China as being a great threat. What kind of a threat?

China's best single customer is the U.S.; and the U.S. purchases more from China than from any other nation. Why would they bomb us?

The two main conflict areas seem to be 1. **economic competition** (from China, this land of 1.4 billion, people who are capable of manufacturing anything, and doing it at less cost than the U.S. does with its 346 million people) and 2. **military expansion**; China has a military base in Djibouti, that's it. So the oligarchs are scared, and they have managed to scare the U.S. government.

Recall what Roosevelt said about the U.S. government-". . . that a financial element in the large centers has owned the government of the United States since the days of Andrew Jackson." Or, in Einstein's words, "An oligarchy of *private* capital the enormous power of which cannot be effectively checked even by a democratically organized political society".

"Then came Citizens United, the Supreme Court's 5-4 First Amendment decision in 2010 that extended to corporations for the first time full rights to spend money as they wish in candidate elections — federal, state and local. The decision reversed a century of legal understanding, unleashed a flood of campaign cash and created a crescendo of controversy that continues to build today." [NPR, JULY 28, 2014] But the oligarchs are happy.

"The trouble with America is that when the dollar only earns 6 percent over here, then it gets restless (***and competitive***) and goes overseas to get 100 percent. Then the flag follows the dollar and the soldiers follow the flag." [General Butler], italics of RW]. And before you know it… The U.S. has some 700 or more military bases *in at least 70 countries and territories (2024)*.***Who is responsible?*** American 2024 elections have just been completed. We shall see who will benefit from all the money in American politics. War is not essential. Surely we can do better!

Reconsider Einstein's opinion on page 31.

"Peace is not just the absence of conflict; peace is the creation of an environment where all can flourish, Nelson Mandela

"America can do whatever we set our mind to." —Barack Obama

"I have known war as few men now living know it. Its very destructiveness on both friend and foe has rendered it useless as a means of settling international disputes." —General Douglas MacArthur

"All peoples are solely tired of the fear, destruction, and the waste of war. As never before, the world knows the human and material costs of war and seeks to replace force with a genuine role of law among nations." —President Eisenhower, State of the Union message, January 9, 1959

Justice
Justice in the hands of the powerful is merely a governing system like any other.
Why call it justice? Let us rather call it injustice, but of a sly effective order,
based entirely on cruel knowledge of the resistance of the weak,
their capacity for pain, humiliation and misery.
Injustice sustained at the exact degree of necessary tension to turn the cogs of the huge
machine-for-the-making-of-rich-men, without bursting the boiler.

Georges Bernanos (1888–1948), French novelist, political writer.
—M. Olivier, in The Diary of a Country Priest, Ch. 7 (1936)

"But it was impossible to save the Great Republic.
She was rotten to the heart.
Lust of conquest had long ago done its work;
trampling upon the helpless abroad had taught her,
by a natural process, to endure with apathy the like at home;
multitudes who had applauded the crushing of other people's liberties,

lived to suffer for their mistake in their own persons.
The government was irrevocably in the hands of the prodigiously rich and their hangers-on;
the suffrage was become a mere machine, which they used as they chose.
There was no principle but commercialism, no patriotism but of the pocket."

— Mark Twain (Samuel Clemens), 19th-century American humorist,
author and journalist. In his: *Letters from the Earth*

Since 1945 have there been any world conflicts which could have justified the use of nuclear weapons? Are there any American politicians that you would trust with the responsibility of using nuclear weapons? Could you trust anyone in the world with this responsibility? Is there any one, any cabal, qualified to make such a decision? It might be wise to remove the necessity for such decisions from human hands and minds.

PHOTOGRAPHS: People caught in Nuclear War.

CAUTION: The following five photographs have been described by an American educator as gruesome and disturbing. These photographs have been viewed and studied by more than 20 million Japanese schoolchildren, visitors to the Hiroshima Peace Museum. My own students over the past 53 years have greatly appreciated seeing and learning the truth about nuclear war, regardless of the difficulties accompanying the truth. Don't let yourself be misled by people who say of our adversaries, "Nuke 'em." It usually affects the citizens and children in the cities, not the mad villains. A small primitive nuclear bomb killed about 140,000 humans by December 31, 1945 in Hiroshima. Nagasaki lost 73,884 to the bomb by the end of 1945.

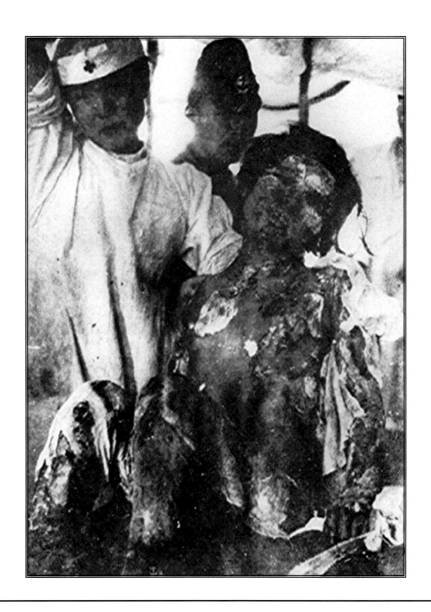

14 year old girl of Nagasaki. Shall this be the fate of our children, or the children of any nation? Dr. Shiotsuki said, "My first assignment was mercy killing." Permission from the widow of Dr. Masao Shiotsuki, via Kosei Publishing.

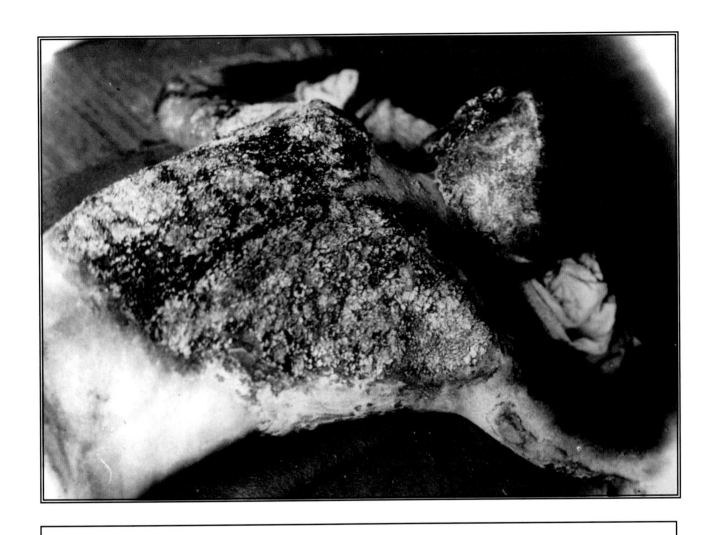

In Japan the bomb was described as "thermic."
Little did they suspect what would next happen to the more than 210,000 victims.
(Taken by Gonichi Kimura), Code HP 143,
Courtesy of the Hiroshima Peace Memorial Museum Curatorial Division
Please do not reproduce without permission.

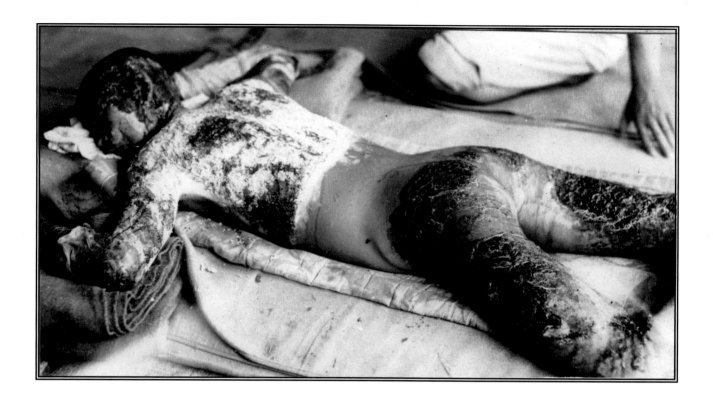

This burn is clearly from the flash of the Hiroshima bomb. His skin where it was covered was not burned. Contrast this with images of a body completely burned; such victims may have been burned by the bomb's flash but afterward they were caught up in the conflagration of the entire city. Who will next use a nuclear weapon on a city? (Taken by Masami Onuka) Code SA002-2, Courtesy of the Hiroshima Peace Memorial Museum Curatorial Division.

Pleas do not reproduce without permission.

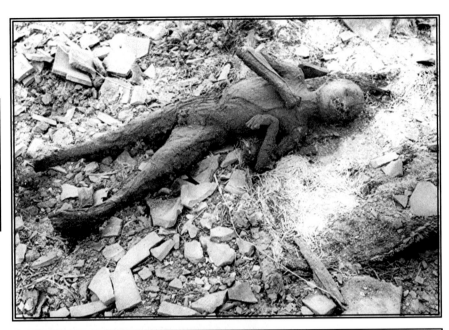

Boy's photo A-13—20, by YosukeYamahata, © Shigo Yamahata.

Girl's photo permission from Nagasaki City.

Notes

* **"Twenty-Four Eyes"**. Original title "**Nijushi no hitomi**", 1954, 156 minutes.

Directed by Keisuke Kinoshita, Starring Hideko Takamine. Written by Keisuke Kinosita and Sakae Tsuboi.

Twenty-Four Eyes was released in Japan by Shochiku on 15 September 1954, where it received generally positive reviews and was a commercial success. It received numerous awards, including the <u>Blue Ribbon Award</u>, the <u>Mainichi Film Award</u> and the <u>Kinema Junpo Award for Best Film of 1954</u>, and the <u>Golden Globe Award</u>. **And it has Wilson's recommendation.**

Based on the novel, **"Twenty-Four Eyes" by Sakae Tsuboi**. Produced by Ryotaro Kuwata. Cinematography by Hiroshi Kusuda. Edited by Yoshi Sugihara. Music by Chuji Kinoshita. Distributed by Shochiku. **Language is Japanese, usually with subtitles.**

Because the teacher's surname Ōishi (大石) can be translated as "Big Stone", but she is shorter in stature than her predecessor, the children address her as "Miss Pebble" (小石, Koishi).

Look for the "Twenty-Four Eyes Movie Studio" in the Google map of the Japanese Island, Shodoshima. Also, along the road just before you reach that site, in the village Tanoura is the caption, "Movie location of 24 hitomi-school location"; use the Enter Street View drag and picture dots will show up on one building, the original school rooms. From the street you can enter the courtyard. Have fun!

1. Sumiteru Taniguchi, THE ATOMIC BOMB ON MY BACK, A Life Story of Survival and Activism, Compiled by Tomokuni Hisashi, Rootstock Publishing, 2020. ISBN: 978-1-57869-040-4
   See also: Peter Townsend, THE POSTMAN OF NAGASAKI, The Story of a Survivor, Collins, London, UK,
   1984, ISBN: 978-0002170673

2. J. Robert Oppenheimer, "*THE INTERNATIONAL CONTROL OF ATOMIC ENERGY,*" Bulletin of the Atomic Scientists, Vol. 1, June, p. 1-5, 1946. Reprinted in THE ATOMIC BOMB, H. W. Wilson Co., New York, 1946.

3. HIROSHIMA JOE, by Martin Booth, Picador, NY, 1985. p.361 and p.390.

4. In a solicitation letter from the Emergency Committee of Atomic Scientists, Nov. 29, 1947. Some of the other Committee Trustees were: Hans Bethe, Harold Urey, Linus Pauling, Leo Szilard, Frederick Seitz, and Victor Weisskopf.

5. Carroll Quigley, TRAGEDY AND HOPE: A HISTORY OF THE WORLD IN OUR TIME, Macmillan, 1966. [GSG & Associates] ISBN-10: 094500110X.

6. Why Socialism?, *Monthly Review*, Vol. 1, No. 1, May, 1949 and repeatedly republished in MR.. https://monthlyreview.org/2009/05/01/why-socialism/

7. Martin Cohen, 101 Ethical Dilemmas, Routledge, 2nd Edition, 2004, p. 258.

8. www.nytimes.com/2003/07/06/books/chapters/what-every-person-should-know-about-war.html

9. J. Robert Oppenheimer, "*THE INTERNATIONAL CONTROL OF ATOMIC ENERGY*," Bulletin of the Atomic Scientists, Vol. 1, June, p. 1-5, 1946. Reprinted in THE ATOMIC BOMB, H. W. Wilson Co., New York, 1946.

10. Philip Morrison and Kostas Tsipis, REASON ENOUGH TO HOPE, MIT Press, 1998.

11. Naomi Shohno, THE LEGACY OF HIROSHIMA – Its Past, Our Future, Kosei Publishing Co., Tokyo, 1986, page 135. ISBN 4-333-01234-1 (Not to be confused with a book by Edward Teller and Allen Brown.)

12. James C. Warf, ALL THINGS NUCLEAR, Figueroa Press, 2005.

13. All member nations are required to abide by the Charter, and they have agreed to do so by signing the Charter when they joined the United Nations.

The Purposes of the United Nations are:

❶ To maintain international peace and security, and to that end: to take effective collective measures for the prevention and removal of threats to the peace, and for the suppression of acts of aggression or other breaches of the peace, and to bring about by peaceful means, and in conformity with the principles of justice and international law, adjustment or settlement of international disputes or situations which might lead to a breach of the peace; ❷ To develop friendly relations among nations based on respect for the principle of equal rights and self-determination of peoples, and to take other appropriate measures to strengthen universal peace;

?To achieve international cooperation in solving international problems of an economic, social, cultural, or humanitarian character and in promoting and encouraging respect for human rights and for fundamental freedoms for all without distinction as to race, sex, language, or religion; and ❹ To be a centre for harmonizing the actions of nations in the attainment of these common ends.

14. Parameters, Summer 1997, pages 4–8, publisher United States Army War College "Constant Conflict". **https://press.armywarcollege.edu/cgi/viewcontent.cgi?article=1829&context=parameters**

15. 15. Andrei Sakharov, 1973 interview, **https://www.csmonitor.com/1984/0619/061946.html** https://news.hrvh.org/veridian/?a=d&d=vcmisc19860418-01.2.7&e=-------en-20--1--txt-txIN-------

16. Michael Parenti, THE FACE OF IMPERIALISM, Paradigm Publishers, Boulder, CO, 2011.

17. W. Cleon Skousen's THE NAKED CAPITALIST, Buccaneer Books; 1998. ISBN-10: 0899683231

18. James C. Warf, ALL THINGS NUCLEAR, Figueroa Press, 2005.

19. Ichiro Kawasaki, THE JAPANESE ARE LIKE THAT, Charles E. Tuttle Co., 1955.

20. Gerald E. Marsh & George S Stanford, *BATTERIES INCLUDED*, Bulletin of the Atomic Scientists, Nov/Dec, 2006, p. 19. (More information via the Internet, e.g., **http://www.fas.org/faspir/2001/v54n5/nuclear.htm**) **https://journals.sagepub.com/doi/full/10.2968/062006006**

21. Marilyn Waring, Documentary *'Who's Counting'*, based on her book, COUNTING FOR NOTHING, University of Toronto Press, 1999.

22. Spencer Weart, NEVER AT WAR: WHY DEMOCRACIES WILL NOT FIGHT ONE ANOTHER, Yale University Press, 2000.

23. World Military Spending
    http://www.globalissues.org/article/75/world-military-spending

Epilogue

Working & Parenting at the Memorial Cenotaph for the
A-Bomb Victims in Hiroshima Peace Park, 1992. . Within the Peace Park Cenotaph is
a vault containing the names of all known victims of the atomic bombing.
More names are added each year.

About the Author:

Professor Wilson has involved himself in these matters since 1959 when he was asked to teach high school physics students about nuclear war and their safety. (You were out of luck if you did not take physics.)

Among Amazon reviews of his earlier writings one finds:

Referring to the E-book, '**Nuclear War: Hiroshima, Nagasaki, and A Workable Moral Strategy for Achieving and Preserving World Peace**' 2014, "It is a must read for anybody that has the slightest interest in the events of Hiroshima and Nagasaki. The author's knowledge is one of the deepest I have ever encountered on the topic. Also, the recommendations for a sensible path moving forward are very much worth the read. Highly recommend." (2024: *The E-book is being revised and updated.*)

"The solution proposed for the Israel-Palestine conflict is extremely ingenious and definitely worth thinking about. Seemingly impossible at first, it shows just the kind of out of the box creativity, needed to solve these complicated problems."

"If you care about the future of your children and grandchildren, - read this book."

". . . thinking Americans deserve a reminder that nuclear war is a ghastly, civilization-ending possibility that goes beyond any special effects that Hollywood can create."

Raymond G. Wilson is an emeritus professor of Physics who has taught about nuclear physics, Hiroshima and Nagasaki for 53 years. In addition to his yearly assignments he has spent 18 summers in Hiroshima and Nagasaki, exploring, meeting people, learning, and writing about their nuclear catastrophes; all done with his super-aide wife, Akiko. He created a physics course in 1979, "Problems of Nuclear Disarmament" that became quite popular; taught it for 33 years, stopping at age 80.

In the early 2000s he led a series of five summer one-week workshops, "Hiroshima and Nagasaki for Teachers." These workshops were partly supported by the program, Science Education for New Civic Engagements and Responsibilities, (SENCER) of the Association of American Colleges and Universities (AAC&U). The workshops had primary support at their inception and beyond from Nagasaki City and Hiroshima Mayor Akiba's program to establish peace-study courses throughout the world. That program was administered by the Hiroshima Peace Culture Foundation located in the extraordinary Hiroshima Peace Memorial Museum. In the U.S. and in Japan Wilson has made more than 40 contributions in print or in person concerning the topics of this inspiring "Incentivization" book.

Printed in the United States
by Baker & Taylor Publisher Services